T0115052

The King

by My Side

A Celebration of Love and Loyalty

Kerry A. Loeffler

BALBOA.
PRESS

A DIVISION OF HAY HOUSE

Balboa Press books may be ordered through booksellers or by contacting:

Balboa Press
A Division of Hay House
1663 Liberty Drive
Bloomington, IN 47403
www.balboapress.com
1 (877) 407-4847

Because of the dynamic nature of the Internet, any web addresses or
links contained in this book may have changed since publication and
may no longer be valid. The views expressed in this work are solely those
of the author and do not necessarily reflect the views of the publisher,
and the publisher hereby disclaims any responsibility for them.

The author of this book does not dispense medical advice or prescribe the use
of any technique as a form of treatment for physical, emotional, or medical
problems without the advice of a physician, either directly or indirectly. The
intent of the author is only to offer information of a general nature to help you
in your quest for emotional and spiritual well-being. In the event you use any
of the information in this book for yourself, which is your constitutional right,
the author and the publisher assume no responsibility for your actions.

Any people depicted in stock imagery provided by Thinkstock are models,
and such images are being used for illustrative purposes only.
Certain stock imagery © Thinkstock.

Printed in the United States of America.

ISBN: 978-1-4525-8635-9 (sc)
ISBN: 978-1-4525-8634-2 (hc)
ISBN: 978-1-4525-8633-5 (e)

Library of Congress Control Number: 2013920438

Balboa Press rev. date: 03/18/2014

Dedication

This book was written in honor of a friend who proved himself true. I love you King. Thank you. Thank you for teaching me the truth.

This book was also written on behalf of all the animals on Earth and for every person who loves them. I hope this book, King's book, will be a light for them, illuminating what once was in shadow.

Introduction

This is a love story. Not a tale of romance, but a story of love nonetheless. Within its words is woven a story of divinity, truth and unconditional love between my beloved cat King and myself.

As a child, I felt a meaningful connection to and a loving compassion for animals. My imagination qualified and inspired my innocent attempts to communicate with them. I whistled to birds on my walks home from school, delivered mental messages to the deer I spied in the woods and whispered softly to my pets as we snuggled in bed before sleep.

As it often happens, adulthood stole away my imagination. My innocent thinking and beliefs in fairytales vanished when the world around me dictated that animal communication was a nonsensical impossibility. All whistling, whispering and mental messages halted as I embraced the world of logic and critical thinking.

In my mid twenties, I experienced an event that once again demanded a paradigm shift from me. In the midst of a voyage of self-discovery, spiritual awakening and a spontaneous opening of my heart and mind, I heard my good friend and beloved cat

King speak to me for the first time. This time it was not childlike imagination! Thus, an earnest journey began and an inspired discovery of truth and love followed. This is that story. It is a true account of my adventures with an animal companion who inspired me to embrace the world of Spirit and taught me to believe in impossible fairytales again. On our path to healing together, King proved to be a loving and wise counselor, the most loyal of friends and an advocate for all animals on Earth. His life has changed mine forever, and hopefully, will change yours too.

Preface

All animals are divine creatures of God. The same divinity that runs through you and me runs through them. They are so openly connected to Spirit, virtually unclouded by ego, that they are living in a state of oneness with all that is. They are in complete harmony with God's spiritual truths.

Animals have an innate and beautiful potential to show us a greater understanding of ourselves and the love from which we all flow. They are gifts of absolute love, sent by Spirit, to bring us joy, to teach us and to love and be loved. By reflecting and mirroring us, they show us our greatest strengths and our darkest weaknesses. In doing so, they heal us.

Animals love us unconditionally, as Spirit does. They have no harsh judgments for us as their keepers. They see and know our potential for spiritual advancement. Part of their purpose, here on Earth, is assisting us to achieve that potential.

Animals can forgive us for our transgressions against them, for their hearts are so open. However, they do not forget. Our companions are capable of the same array of rich emotions as we are. They all have the potential for great suffering and overwhelming joy. They experience life with as much, and sometimes more, awareness as we do. Every act of injustice towards them is felt entirely. When basic needs are not met, or when treatment of them is less than they deserve, their suffering is real. When we return their love for us with kindness and gratitude, their joy is real. They deserve to be respected and acknowledged for all that they are. They are waiting for us to wake up, listen and see them in truth.

Moe

At the age of fourteen, a time when childhood ends and the world begins to take new meaning, the dawning of adulthood beckoned to me with one tiny miracle. My mother decided it was time to get a new kitty. Our former cat had been missing for weeks. We had finally given up hope that he would return. With the feeling of loss so fresh, I was hesitant about adopting a new cat; unsure of loving anything ever again.

Nervously, I rode with Mom to the Iosco County Animal Shelter. We were greeted with abundant and eager voices, all barking, meowing and whining in unison. Instantly overcome with sorrow and concern, I choked back my tears. How many innocent animals would be put down? Desperation seized me as I looked at all of their little faces; why could I not save all of them? If one life was all that could be saved that day, I rationalized that we had better save an older cat who would be less likely to escape euthanasia. A kitten would more likely steal a heart and find a home.

My mother had a different idea. She was standing in front of a cage overflowing with kittens, smiling with delight.

"Mom, let's get this one." I motioned toward an older, gray cat, "Nobody will want him."

"Hmm… you think so?" Her gaze stayed with the kittens. "What about this little gray tiger with white paws? He looks like he's wearing a tuxedo."

"I guess so." It was pointless to argue with Mom.

I whispered, "Good luck", to the older cat and regretfully shuffled over to the kittens. Mom was now holding a tiny, gray, tiger kitten in her hands. His bright green eyes spied me from behind her palms.

Mom had chosen our new kitty. The choice was made so quickly, so naturally, without debate. In that instant, a wheel set into motion for me, though I could not know it at the time. That kitten would have a powerful impact on every part of me, down to the very fibers of my soul. He would open me in ways I never dreamed. He would teach me like an elder teaches a youth. He would change me forever, blessing me with a greater understanding of Spirit and all of its creations.

Mom paid the shelter attendant two dollars and we were off. As it turned out, we got quite the deal that day. In time, this little kitten's true value would be revealed.

My eyes were red with worry. We left so many sweethearts behind. Would they find homes? Would they have a chance to be loved?

"Why are you crying Kerry?" Mom asked.

"I'm not crying. It's my allergies."

My attention soon switched to the soft fur now tickling the back of my neck. Our new little kitty had crawled up my chest, nestled himself in the nape of my neck and was hiding under my hair. His purring was louder than any I had ever heard. Wow, he was a cutie! He stole my heart immediately. I fell in love hard and fast. Somewhere inside, I knew this one was different. He was special. The bliss of our immediate connection instantaneously voided my fears of loving again.

Perhaps I felt our destiny. Two puzzle pieces had locked together, our lives linked in perfect time and space. All I knew was that this kitty was mine, we were meant to be with each other!

Mom glanced over at me from the driver's seat and asked, "What's his name?"

"Moe."

Moe and I fell right into rhythm together. He slept in my bed every night, starting from the first. He was such a happy little kitten. I could not have known then how grateful he was for his new home and for me. That was something he would share with me later, when we were at a much, much different time in our lives.

It soon became obvious to the rest of the members of my family that Moe really was tied to me. We were in harmony; linked together like kindred spirits. Our connection was evident. My little sister was just a bit jealous. I teased her every chance I could: "Moe is my kitty, not yours!"

A few weeks later, another new friend arrived. Dad was in the garage cleaning his latest catch of fish. He was not happy about my new best friend. Mom had been masquerading Moe as a birthday present for Dad. However, we all knew that was not the truth. Dad's birthday was just an excuse to bring a new kitty home. He had an aversion to cats due to his allergies. We had often witnessed his sneezing fits.

So there Dad was, cleaning fish, probably grumbling to himself about Mom always getting what she wanted, when little Heather Feather toddled in. She was no older than six weeks, a tiny, little mess. She was cold, wet, dirty and scared. The poor thing even had a bad case of ear mites. Who knows how long she was surviving in the woods before the smell of fish brought her to us?

My jaw hit the floor when Dad walked in with that petite, peeping kitten and announced, loud and proud, "Look what I found! We are keeping her. Her name is Heather." I'll never know why he chose to keep her. He never wanted any other cat. Maybe she just played his heartstrings. Whatever the reason, she had impeccable timing. Appealing her case to Dad definitely worked in her favor. She had found her new home.

My sister jumped for joy. "She's mine, she's mine!"

Moe and Heather did not have the usual spats over sharing their home. Their meeting was even romantic. We cleaned her up and then let Moe perform his inspection. Before long, Moe's sniffing turned to licking and Heather was receiving her second bath of the night. She was relieved and basked in the attention. He cleaned her until they were both satisfied and then they fell asleep in each other's arms. It was as if they recognized each other, as if they were long, lost friends. We all wondered if it was love at first sight.

We frequently found Moe and Heather lying in each other's arms. When they were not out hunting and playing, they were snuggling in front of the patio doors. There they would lick, hug, clean and love each other. They were living in the lap of feline luxury; blessed with an abundance of mice to hunt, a warm home, loving humans and, of course, each other. After their humble and meager beginnings, they were happy to enjoy their newfound paradise.

Moe and Heather enjoyed a privileged life together for a time. They caught mice, took baths and napped together before retiring to their separate beds in the evening, Heather to my sister's and Moe to mine.

Then, one night a few years later, Heather did not come home. Moe looked for her. He called and cried. We all called and cried. No answer came, Heather never returned and we never knew why. We had our theories: maybe an owl, a hawk, a coyote. There was nothing we could do. My sister cried and cried. So did Moe.

Moe loved Heather so much, his grief was discernible. Was the old adage true? Was it really better to have loved and lost than to never have loved at all? A piece of Moe's heart went with Heather, a hole I would find later.

Life carried on despite our devastation. Moe kept catching mice and leaving them in the most strategic places. He loved to bring us presents. One particular night, I had an argument with Mom. I was sitting at the table, a frustrated teenager irritated with her unreasonable rules. Moe popped his head through the cat door, looked at me proudly and dropped a dead mouse on the floor. Mom was in the shower, the mouse would be in her direct path when she walked out of the bathroom. How brilliantly awful and gruesome, it was just the revenge I was seeking.

As Mom exited the bathroom, I casually neglected to mention Moe's well-crafted surprise. She hit it square! Her bare, squeaky clean, foot squished directly on top of the dead mouse! Vengeance was mine!

Being very careful to conceal my joy, I carried my friend up to my room where we could celebrate unnoticed. Hugging my friend tightly in my arms, I whispered, "Thanks Moe! You are so awesome. Nice to know you've got my back."

Moe used several of his nine lives in those early years. He spent a few escaping the wrath of Mom after such sticky situations. He once ate a steak she had set out to thaw and barely escaped with his life. Another time, he was hiding on top of the open garage door. He panicked when the door began to close. There was nowhere to run. Without my quick-thinking father, who reflexively stopped the door, he surely would have met his demise.

Another day, I heard him screaming as I approached the house from the school bus. My hands dropped my bags and my feet carried me home faster than my brain could register what was happening. In a total state of panic, I searched and searched through the house, but could not find the source of the screams. They were becoming louder and more terrified, still Moe was nowhere to be found.

After what seemed like forever, I calmed myself and focused harder on the source of the shrill sounds. The cries sounded like they were coming from the upstairs bath, but I had already looked there. I flew up the stairs and past the door to the bathroom. Moe screamed again. He was not in the bathroom! There was no sign of him, yet the screams were right there. Without a thought, my hand opened the small door to the laundry chute. My eyes swelled with the sight of my dearest friend, clinging to the edge of the chute and to dear life. Below him was a fall, three flights down, to the concrete basement floor. My arms deftly snatched my sweetheart from danger, prying his claws from the wooden frame of the laundry chute, and held him close to my chest and heart.

"Moe! How the hell did you do that? How long were you hanging there? Thank God I got you!" He clung to me in relief. For at least a minute, he held on close, until the panic left his body.

After his heartbeat slowed, and our embrace was sufficient enough to erase his fear, I kissed his forehead and whispered, "you are safe, buddy. I hope that wasn't your last life." He jumped from my arms and casually began licking and cleaning himself of the stress. Silently, I thanked God that I was able to deliver him from the danger of a terrible fall.

Three years later, it was time for me to go to college. Moe came with me to my first apartment in the city. A month went by before I realized that the city was no place for a country cat. One evening, I noticed Moe sitting quietly, staring at me. It was as if he was attempting to burn a message into my brain. I stared back, wondering what he was communicating. Then I got it: he was bored and unhappy; he needed to be in the woods.

"Okay Love, I'll take you back." Although I would miss him, I knew it was for the best. After all, loving someone is the act of doing what makes them happy. The next week, he was patrolling his old forest and home again.

Two years later, he came to live with me on a permanent basis. We had a big house with a couple of new college roommates.

Behind our house was a small forest, it was just enough to keep Moe the hunter contented.

It was lovely to have my boy back. My friends and roommates enjoyed him too. We received so many compliments on "what a cool cat he was". His popularity became even more apparent during my senior year. One evening at a keg party, I was talking with a friend and drinking flat, warm beer, when Moe strutted in.

"Moe! What are you doing here?"

My friend's mouth fell open, "That's your cat? He is so cool! He comes over all the time!"

"Yup that's my Moe. He is pretty cool."

We had a great time all through our college years. I wonder if he attended as many parties as I did.

While in college, I went away on several trips. My friends were always there to watch him. The instructions for his care were simple: keep the food and water full and leave his window open so he can come and go as he pleases. He was so wise and so clever; there were never any doubts about leaving him. We had sincere trust in each other. I knew if I allowed him ultimate freedom, his spirit would soar. It did.

Moe was well equipped to avoid danger. We had already addressed my worst fear when he was just a kitten. By the edge of the road, in my arms, he learned of the peril of cars. He considered my sincere pleas to stop, look and listen before crossing and the lesson stuck with him.

Shortly after graduation, I took another one of my trips. This time I left my kitty with a new boyfriend in a new apartment. It gave them time to bond, although Moe never did like him. The boyfriend, on the other hand, had decided rather quickly that, "Moe was a pretty cool cat".

Moe had successfully changed Steve's preconceptions about felines in two short days. Steve learned that cats were a joy and a pleasure to be with, something he had never been open to before. Moe learned that Steve was not a joy and pleasure to be with, something I would learn later.

While I was away, tragedy struck. My arm was badly broken in an accident. My mother and boyfriend rushed to Chicago to fetch me from the hospital. My humerus bone was broken into three pieces and my shoulder was dislocated. A titanium rod and nine pins were my only option to put it all back together. After surgery, the Doctors informed me that I may never move that arm again.

A disaster can sometimes serve a great purpose by setting a person on their path. That accident was no accident. It was fate beckoning me to follow my life's mission. At the time, I could only understand that this experience was all dark and painful. There was no silver lining on the cloud of depression and pain hanging over me. Petrified by the thought that I would never be able to use my arm again, I ate as many pain pills as I was allowed. It seemed that this tragedy was one that would not allow recovery.

My recovery was long, but not impossible. The wounds I sustained were a necessary part of my life's purpose. They were vital to understanding the path to healing, a path I had unknowingly just begun.

The physical therapists splinted my hand with this scary-looking contraption meant to hold my wrist and fingers in an anatomically correct position. I jokingly called it my Freddy

Krueger hand and it drew lots of attention. My attempts at humor failed to make a difference in the reactions it collected. People responded to it with a kind of curious nausea. They wanted to ask about it but couldn't. Even so, they would not look away until their eyes got their fill. The stares were hurtful; they pushed me deeper into a spiral of despair.

One afternoon, I was lying on the couch, staring at the mechanical monstrosity on my arm, when my tears began to spill. I wept and my tears soaked the pillow completely. They were endless. Alone and scared, I re-lived the accident. The trauma was having its way with me. My mind and body were writhing in anguish, I was losing the battle.

Moe came out of hiding. He approached the couch where I was lying. His big, green eyes stared into my soul for a moment. Then my little friend jumped up and settled on my chest, covering my heart with his. He looked into my eyes and began purring. I petted him with the one hand I could still move. The thought that I may never pet or hug him with two arms again pushed more tears onto my pillow. That did not matter to my boy. Unscathed by my fears, he continued with his devoted attention, beaming love into my heart. His efforts calmed me and I soon fell into a restful sleep, lulled by the sound of his little motor running.

The comfort and love my friend sent me that day strengthened our bond and gave me a greater appreciation for him. There was more to Moe than I had known before. As I pondered his behavior that day, I realized that he was cognizant of my feelings and felt compassion for me. He had delivered love, from his heart to mine, directly, without words, without pain pills, without jokes and without chicken soup. His heart to heart interaction was issued with a definite and recognizable intention: he loved me dearly.

After some time spent in physical therapy, my arm began to move again. With that, most of my fear subsided. However, I still had a long road to recovery. We decided to move to an apartment on Lake St. Clair. A change of scene sometimes inspires a change of heart. In my case, it was much needed.

Adjacent to our yard was a small patch of trees and ferns positively brimming with mice. Moe caught so many that it became a daily chore to remove them from our front doorstep. This was never my favorite job. Disgusting as it was, I was thrilled that he was happy.

By that time, Moe was eight and I was twenty-two. We had lived over one third of our lives together. My new understanding of Moe's love for me and the way he had responded to my injuries and depression inspired me to investigate his awareness more keenly. I watched him study people from the corner of the room. It seemed as if he was listening to conversations and observing body language. It became easy to discern whether a particular human met his approval. He would happily greet some. Others he snubbed with a flick of his tail as he walked away. I began to trust his instincts and pair them with my own. He was always right. He always knew whom to trust and who had bad intentions. On most occasions, his instincts proved to be much better than mine.

At the same time, I began to notice Moe's intuition, I also made a resolution to pay attention to my own. Listening to the voice in my head was my new, top priority. This voice had been there my entire life and I had no idea what it was. It was always calm, assuring and patient. It always guided me during times of extreme stress. It's warning to me the night I broke my arm had echoed in my head every day since the accident. Moments before my arm was so severely broken, time just stopped, a premonition of overwhelming pain shot down my left limb and a very loud male voice asked me gently, "Kerry, do you still want to go on?" I answered the voice without knowing what it was really asking, without recognizing the painful and difficult journey ahead. My answer was simply, "yes." By rational reason it was the only choice; not going on meant giving up my life. I never told anyone about it; it was my own secret curiosity.

My resolution to listen and pay heed to the voice came after yet another consequence of not listening. I had finally pulled the last straw, the voice that was always right would never again fall on deaf ears. Sitting alone in my living room one evening, I clearly heard the voice say, "Move that glass of water." I obstinately refused to move anything, including my position on the couch. In the next few moments, I bumped the table, knocked the glass over and spilled water all over. The mess was minimal, my irritation was not.

The mess was enough to grab my attention and spark a change. There were times, in the past, when I had chosen to ignore the persistent guidance of the unknown voice. Those occasions had resulted in big, terrible messes that created undue suffering. In that moment, I vowed to always listen and take instruction to the best of my abilities. Though I did not understand who or what this voice was, I trusted it would help me avoid any future messes, large or small. With that seemingly small choice, a journey of self-discovery, that would continue for the rest of my life, began.

Living by the lake was a great place to tune in to my intuitions. The quiet, repetitive lapping of the waves calmed my emotions and quieted my mind. Moe and I were as contented as we could be until the day came when he came close to death. While I was away, on another one of my mini-trips, Moe's care was entrusted to Steve, my live-in boyfriend. I was sure everything would be fine. It always was.

When I arrived home, I popped in the front door and searched the living room for my sweetheart. As soon as I saw Moe I screamed to Steve, "What did you do to my cat?"

Moe's condition was dire. His eyes were glazed, his fur was pale and dusty. He was extremely lethargic and absolutely dazed. I dropped everything and bolted to my ailing friend. My inspection of him uncovered an oily spot on his back just above his tail.

"Steve, you asshole! What did you do?"

His response infuriated me: "I put flea drops on him. I could not take it any more. Our house is infested."

My voice was then screaming at the top of its range. "You know I would never put that toxic, poisonous shit on him! You waited until I left to do it! What the hell did you use?" I recovered the box from the trash and discovered it contained Malathion, a very toxic industrial pesticide. I had just read about it in Rachel Carson's book "Silent Spring". There are toxic waste dumps in Mexico filled with it. The Malathion leaches into the drinking water of nearby villages and causes severe birth defects. It was outlawed as a landscaping pesticide in the United States years after Carson's book hit the shelves. The fact that it was ever considered safe to use on animals is testimony of the careless ethics of the pet care industry.

Steve had given Moe a double dose in the wrong place. Moe was able to lick it up from his lower back and had obviously ingested enough to poison him.

There was no time to rush him to a veterinarian. We did not even have one, until then we never had any need. Instinctually, I threw Moe in the tub. He had no energy to fight it. I washed him with castile soap several times. Moe was mad and that was too bad. I was mad and that was too bad for Steve. Moe was not the only one in hot water!

No wonder Moe did not like Steve. He was a selfish, inconsiderate prick! He had almost killed my best friend! Once again, I realized Moe's instincts about people were entirely accurate.

After his bath, my exhausted friend rested on a towel and licked the excess water out of his fur. An hour later, his condition had improved drastically; he ate a little and fell asleep. The bath and all the water ingested while grooming his wet fur flushed the toxins through his body and saved his life. This was the second time Moe's life was saved and I thanked God again. How many lives were we on now?

The next day, I decided to attack Steve's pile of laundry that had been festering for six months. Just for principle, I had refused to touch it. My resolve had fizzled away and I could not take it any longer. The flea problem was magically solved after the incredible mound of dirty clothes disappeared. Steve's pile of laundry was doing double time as a source of arguments and as a home for fleas. Ironically, the one who needed a dose or two of flea drops was Steve not Moe.

Steve's constant inconsiderate attitude soon drove me to leave him. Moe and I took refuge in a camper trailer set up in my Mom's backyard. Moe loved it; we were in the great North Woods again. The first morning of our stay, I stepped down from our camper and was greeted by my buddy. He was just returning from a night of hunting. He was positively aglow, invigorated by his new surroundings. Just as he had in his early years, there were acres of forest to explore. His joyous expression confirmed that I had made the right decision by leaving Steve. We were on the brink of a new beginning.

Two months later, it was time for an even bigger change. I was not happy with life; the accident that broke my arm had left emotional and physical scars. I bought a new car and took off to Colorado motivated by a quest to heal those scars and find my life's purpose.

Colorful Colorado's mountains and rivers were invigorating. A sense of new adventure rejuvenated my zest for living. As soon as I was settled, I flew back to Michigan to retrieve my best friend. His flight was rough. He was uncomfortable in the small cat carrier and the sounds and turbulence from the plane made him very anxious. Despite the bumpy fight, he was happy to be with me again. This time though, there was no forest for him to explore safely. Michigan and Colorado are in stark contrast. Colorado's mountains, heavily forested with pines, are home to a plethora of predators that would be happy to have a kitty for a meal. Moe was safe in the foothills near Ft. Collins, but he was no longer allowed out at night. Regretfully, I informed him of this. I could not bear to be without him, leaving him in Michigan was absolutely not an option. Moe would have to endure a little less freedom. He responded with despondency.

We were both embarking on a new journey. He was eleven now, I was twenty-five. I vowed to find the answers to my life's greatest questions: Who is God? Who is the voice in my head? Was there a purpose behind my accident? How do I make sense of my life? Why am I here? What am I supposed to do? What is this all for?

Colorado turned out to be a great place for a spiritual awakening. I found myself in a community of healers, yogis and all kinds of alternative thinkers. Yoga and meditation became a daily routine. I read as many spiritual books as I could get my hands on. A paradigm shift took place as my mind began to open. My conservative Christian upbringing was losing its hold on my views. My world was changing; I could no longer compartmentalize my experiences into white or black. All of my time spent in self-care and spiritual study was tuning my awareness and belief systems into new heights: impossibilities were becoming possibilities.

A strange thing happened one night when I was having cocktails on my patio with a few friends. Moe was sitting in the chair across from me listening to our conversation, as he often did. We were laughing and carrying on about a concert we had attended a few hours before. I looked up from nearly choking on laughter and noticed a ghost was also sitting with us. He was an older, slender gentleman wearing a gray suit. I thought I had felt something in this house before but I always dismissed it as imagination. I studied the ghost for a minute. He was not hostile at all, like horror movies would suggest. In fact, his energy was quite gentle. I was not scared; it seemed that he just wanted me to be aware of him. I felt very comfortable in his presence.

The next moment had me in complete shock, however. Moe was watching me watch the ghost. Then, I heard a new voice in my head.

"There's a ghost out here with us."

I looked over at my buddy and said with my own inner voice, "I know, I can see him."

"You can hear me?" Moe's voice was smaller than I was used to.

"Yes, I can hear you. Let's go to bed. We have a lot to talk about."

Excusing myself for the evening, I scooped my kitty up in my arms. My friends were a little stunned by my haste. Shocked and stunned myself, I was eager to find out if I really was talking with my cat. We needed to concentrate together.

As we lay in bed together, Moe asked me again, "You can really hear me?"

"Yes honey, I can and I almost don't believe this!"

He began to purr loudly.

My thoughts began to race. The experience seemed impossible. "I have a lot of questions for you, Moe."

"I'm so happy you can hear me!" He was thrilled.

In the next moments, I drifted unintentionally into sleep. As I allowed sleep to take me, I promised Moe and myself that we would talk the next day. We did not. The high vibration and joy from a night of music, laughter and dance had faded away. My heightened inner hearing went with it.

I was disappointed and elated all at once: disappointed because my newfound discovery was so fleeting, elated because I actually heard Moe speak! This inspired my spiritual quest to go into overdrive. How had I heard Moe? What was it about me that allowed me to hear voices? Wait... cats can talk? Ghosts are real? I can see ghosts! I was more open-minded than ever, life was responding to that by bringing me new experiences. My spiritual quest was providing more questions than it was answers.

Moe and I did not speak for a while after that. Discouraging as that was, I still strove to hit that high vibration again.

After a year in our first Colorado home, it was time to move again. This time we landed west of Ft. Collins, Colorado. The voice that was always there guiding me, had been pushing me to "Go to massage school". I had thoughts about going, but every time I mentioned it to someone, I was met with negative feedback.

"You can't do that."

"Bad idea. The market is flooded."

"There's no money there."

Finally, I stopped letting the negative comments of friends and relatives dictate my decision. I did what my heart, intuitions and the mysterious voice told me to do. That fall, I enrolled in massage school. There I met wonderful teachers who validated my newfound abilities to hear and see things. As I learned from those powerful healers, who were normal people with spiritual gifts and insights, I gave permission to myself to let go of skepticism and embrace a world that cannot always be explained by the scientific method. I allowed myself to believe in intuition, metaphysics, the healing power of touch and my own abilities as a sensitive person. Indeed, there is more to this world than meets the eyes.

The first time I laid my hands on a person with healing intention, chills ran through my body. A spontaneous release came from the deepest parts of my spirit. Silent tears poured from me as I worked. My tears were composed of relief and delight that I had finally found my life's purpose. My moment of recognition had come, I understood everything. All of the events and experiences in my life thus far, were in alignment with who I was and what I was supposed to do. The accident, which left me so severely injured, in so many ways, had inspired a quest to heal myself. Without it, I may never have discovered that I was a healer. It was a vital part of a master plan. Acceptance of all that had passed bathed my body, emotions and mind. In my silent release, I whispered, "This is what God wants me to do."

The more I learned the more I wanted to learn. School was very technical. I drank up the anatomy, physiology, and massage theories. What I really thirsted for was an education in energy anatomy. I found it in experience. As I worked with fellow students, I learned to perceive their energetic fields. Bubbles of light escaped from their bodies under my hands. Their private thoughts and comments they spoke in their minds became perceptible. As I listened to their feedback, my clairaudience blossomed. Hot and cold places filled the spaces above their bodies. My mind struggled to assign order to the new reality my tactile senses were exposing.

A blissful peace washed through me as I allowed God to come through me to heal others. My connection with God and the Holy

Spirit became stronger than I had ever dreamed. Clairvoyance, clairaudience and clairsentience were no longer notions without credence. They were real, real in God and real in me. My world was bursting with the bright colors of new discovery. Like a child, everything was new to me. I was eager to explore and enormously grateful to finally have answers, validation and a roadmap for my life's purpose.

By this time, Moe had reached the stately age of thirteen. It had been a while since I cleaned up any mice. It seemed as though his age was starting catch up with him. No longer was he able to negotiate simple jumps. Moe had always enjoyed drinking the water that dripped from the faucet of the bathroom sink. He was lingering longer on the floor before hefting his body up to the counter. With my fresh education in anatomy, I could easily see he was experiencing some joint pain. We began supplementing with glucosamine chondroitin and experimented with an all-natural, whole foods diet. I prepared chicken, rice and carrot meals for him. His dinner regularly smelled better than mine did. Cooking for him did not last long however. Apparently, he was not fond of leftovers and I was not fond of having to cook his meals fresh everyday. I did some research to find the best, prepared food on the market. Every label I read was appalling. Highly recommended food, the food most veterinarians sell in their clinics, is made from junk. Corn is often the first ingredient. The rest is byproducts. This can hardly be considered food. My research concluded that most pet food companies use the leftovers from slaughterhouses. Their focus was profits, not optimum health. I was disgusted having misplaced my trust in a sick, exploitive industry.

After a bit more searching, I found the best pet food on the market at a local feed store. It was an ancestral food, meaning Moe could eat what his body was designed to eat. It contained no byproducts, no corn, no fillers and only high quality ingredients. It was just a bit more expensive and totally worth it. Moe gobbled it up. His coat became softer and shinier and his eyes brightened. The glucosamine was a big success too. After two weeks of supplementing, he began to jump without hesitation again. That was a reason to smile.

Massage school was going very well. My gifts were emerging. My increasing vibration and new awareness of the power of intention were serving me well. I was beginning to hear Moe's voice more often and more clearly. His comments frequently cracked me up. Moe had taught himself to open doors when he was younger. His door opening talents allowed us the convenience of hiding his litter box inside the bathroom cabinets. This arrangement offered him privacy and kept any messes out of view. We were having ourselves a lovely snuggle one afternoon when he jumped up in between strokes. "Where are you going?" I asked.

"To the wall," he answered, excusing himself to the bathroom. I tried not to let him hear me giggle. He turned and gave me an annoyed look.

"I'm sorry, you're just so cute. It is not a wall. It's a cabinet." My giggles were met with admonishment. He did not return to my lap when he was finished, I had insulted his intelligence. He did not appreciate my comments or laughter; they were rather undignified and did not appeal to his royal feline nature.

Tragedy struck again in the spring. This time it really hurt. Fate had delivered another disastrous blow to put me more firmly on my path, and this time Moe on his. We were on the precipice of discovering the powerfully divine purpose of Moe's life. I was about to realize how much love I had for him, and how much love he had for me. This love would shape, form and mold the rest of my days. Soon, I would be humbled and eternally grateful to him.

It was a lovely spring day, school had let out early. Moe and I were drinking up the fresh, crisp air on our back patio. I placed him on the ledge of the railing; he loved the view from there. He lost his balance. His back end was dangling. He struggled to grasp the railing but his front claws were not there to dig into the wood. I ran to catch him but my bike was in the way and I stumbled over it, missing my friend. As he fell, he attempted to twist his body and land on his feet. He hit the concrete, twenty feet below, mid-twist.

I screamed as I flew down the steps, "Moe! No! Oh my God!"

Seconds later, I was scooping him up and surveying his body. There was no blood, no apparent damage. I carried him in the house and put him on the floor. He began eating and purring, his response to stress and pain.

My neighbor, who had come running when he heard my screams, comforted me, "He's fine. He is fine. See, he's eating."

His words were of no value to me, I knew they were not true. Moe's lower vertebrae were noticeably crooked and he could not raise his tail. I called the vet and rushed him in. She took x-rays and found some slight misalignment in his spine. She dismissed us and said there was nothing she could do. She thought his tail was "stuck" because of the stress.

The next day, I awoke with a resolute knowledge that the vet had missed Moe's injury. I just knew it. We went back for more x-rays. This time, I asked her to shoot for the hips and lower spine. There it was. He had dislocated the second to the last vertebra before the tail. Good, I thought, he is not broken.

Moe was lying on the floor of the office as the vet and I discussed the x-ray results. He was scared. He detested vets.

All hope quickly drained from me as the doctor explained that there would be too much pressure on his spine. Her treatment recommendation was to cut off his tail. Moe whipped his head around delivering me a horrified glare. It was clear that he did not agree with her treatment plan.

"Don't worry," I told him secretly, "we are not doing that." The vet was confused by my decision. We left with some steroids and pain medications.

Absolutely wrought with worry, I took Moe into meditation with me. We lied in a crystal grid patterned around my bed. Then, I accessed his energy for the first time, with intentions of healing him. I felt through his aura, petting him just above his body. Completely uncentered and ungrounded, I worked in fear and grief, managing only to remove some pain and impact. Though I washed away every bubble I could find, I knew this was a bad injury, a challenge for even an immensely powerful healer. Only a beginner myself, how could I manage? My skills were just budding, my eyes were just opening, and my understanding of energy and anatomy were still immature.

My energy soon ran out. Giving up, I settled myself inside the crystal grid and carefully placed Moe over my heart. We began to climb to God. I really had no idea what to do or how to do it. What I did know was that any time life gave me something that seemed bigger than me, any time I was scared or overwhelmed, I had always given it to God. This was the only thing I could do in that moment. We lied there climbing energetically through my crown chakra. I was carrying him to God. Moe wanted only to rest, he was hurt and stressed. My combing through his aura and crying over him were completely intolerable. Peacefully breathing together was a much more acceptable effort. We arrived about an hour later, having gone as far up as I could go. We were met with compassion. I sensed the tiniest presence of God looking on us sweetly, thankful and proud that I had brought Moe to him.

That was it. We did not go through the door to heaven and meet God to receive a powerful healing. We were given a smidgeon of grace and a peaceful sleep.

I woke up the next morning confused, disappointed, scared and clueless. Many mornings thereafter had passed in much the same way. Every day after that accident, upon awakening, my first thought was about Moe and his needs. Most mornings my eyes were not even open before stress and fear come flooding into my mind. What was I going to do? How was I going to help my buddy? I had no idea where to take him or what was going to heal him. This injury was far beyond my abilities. Moe needed a miracle. My despair grew stronger and I froze.

Our vet called us days later asking me to reconsider my decision. She had consulted with another, very accomplished, colleague who agreed with her treatment plan. We discussed Moe's condition in detail. If we did not cut off his tail, there was no telling how or if he would recover. If we did cut off his tail, it could alleviate some pressure on his spine and his chance of a full recovery would be improved. Either way there was no guarantee. Even so, she pushed me hard to remove Moe's tail.

I couldn't tell her how Moe felt. She would think I was nuts. My only choice was to advocate for my friend and respect his wishes. Her explanations and persuasions were pointless: Moe did not want to lose his tail, it was his decision. She continued to plead with me. Quietly, I realized conventional medicine was not going to be our answer.

At school the next day, my instructor gave me some time to ask for prayers for my friend. I reminded my fellow students of some words that had often brought comfort and power to unfortunate circumstances in my past; Jesus said, "Whenever there are two or more in prayer, I am there". Hoping that twenty-two people could bring a miracle to my Moe, we all bowed our heads and delivered a payer in unison. When I returned home, there were no noticeable changes. Where was Jesus?

If conventional medicine wasn't our answer, then perhaps energy medicine and massage were the answer. After all, this was where the roadmaps in my life were leading me. I wondered if it all had happened for a reason: since Moe was my responsibility, since his care was in my hands, perhaps my hands were the ones who could heal him. It was possible that I could learn by working with him and there, maybe, we would find healing.

Desperately, I wished the fall had never happened. I had once saved him from the danger of a fall, why not twice? If there was a reason, wasn't there a better way? Loving Moe so much and seeing him in pain was killing me; I longed to see him raise his tail again.

Denial and trepidation grasped me. My fear of failing Moe, as his healer, began to stall our relationship. Every time he jumped on my lap, I felt obligated to heal him with the love that could come through my hands. Then the fear and doubt would take over. They consumed me. When he invited affection, I made attempts at channeling. He just wanted to snuggle. I could not; the pressure I felt to heal him would not allow me. He jumped from my lap time after time out of frustration. We were broken.

Meanwhile, I searched my community for a chiropractor who would work on animals. There were none. Colorado had passed a law that prevented any chiropractor from working with animals without a veterinarian present. This law made the whole concept of chiropractic care for animals very expensive and almost impossible. I begged my own chiropractor to see him. He would not risk his license.

After searching quite a bit, I found one doctor who had retired to his farm. He agreed to adjust Moe, "behind closed doors", for twenty-five dollars. Moe absolutely hated it. He adjusted easily but begrudgingly. After each session, the doctor and I would watch Moe walk around the farm. We searched for changes in his gait. The changes were small; his hips and spine would hold for a day and then fall back to their crooked position.

We did this a few times until the day that the doctor came for a house call. He adjusted Moe and everything was fine except for the feeling I got from the doctor. He seemed desperate somehow and I lost confidence and trust in him. We never saw him after that. Something just was not right.

Two months after the fall, I noticed Moe was missing the litter box. At first, I thought this was just a natural consequence of age. Then, he began peeing everywhere. It didn't make sense. He was a good kitty; he would not do that. All of the messes were cleaned and I made no connections to his injury.

After weeks of cleaning and confusion, I screamed at him, "Moe! Stop peeing everywhere! Why are you doing this?" All of my frustration had mounted; I was in a raging fit.

Moe cried back, "Kerry, I don't know I'm peeing!"

His answer silenced me. At once, I understood. My fit of rage turned into a fountain of tears, "I'm sorry baby, I'm so sorry. I love you so much."

I curled myself up around Moe on the floor of the kitchen, petting him as he ate his food. Silently, I thought about his condition. After a moment, I came to a conclusion. It was conclusion I wanted to neither believe nor share with Moe.

Later that day, I looked up my chart of the spine and nerves. There it was, just as I had feared. The injured vertebrae and intersecting nerves controlled the bladder and bowels. His descent had begun; the nerves were beginning to fail. He was losing bladder control, next would be bowels and then… well, what would happen after that was too awful to ponder. I struggled to hold onto my faith in healing, miracles and the power of God.

A few weeks later, we found a new friend who was very talented at the practice of Healing Touch for animals. She advertised in a small healing publication; I called her the moment I found the ad.

She listened to me closely as I told her about Moe. Her compassion came through the phone. We scheduled right away.

Moe loved her. They would talk telepathically as she worked on him, sometimes while I was in the same room. I heard him complain to her that I would not "pet him just to pet him" anymore. She mentioned this to me after their first session. Her words ripped through me; I loved Moe more than anything I had ever loved and now I was hurting him. After that, I did my best to "just pet" him, but guilt, fear and pressure to heal him pervaded my touch.

Moe always glowed after our new friend's visits. He would lie in his chair, purring, happy and content. It was obvious that he was getting some kind of relief and I loved seeing him like that. However, where were the improvements to his body? Nothing had changed physically and the incontinence persisted.

By this time, I had graduated massage school and was taking weekend trips for energy healing workshops. I always hoped I would learn something that would give me great insight and power to put his body back together. I hoped that I would become such a powerful channel, with my new energetic training, that I could heal Moe completely and we could go back to just being happy again. Upon my return from a particularly powerful weekend, I scooped Moe into my arms and whispered into his ear how much I had missed him.

"You always know how to hold me", he purred.

In between our healer friend's visits, I worked with my buddy as much as I could bring myself to. I was crumbling under the weight of the burden I had placed on myself. Moe did not like the massage table. It was a struggle just to keep him on it. The first few times I worked with him, we focused only on the physical injury. Moe's injured muscles were easy to locate. Unfortunately, his injury left him in quite a bit of pain and even my lightest touch was too much. I kept my hands as soft as I could, he just did not want me in there. He was guarding his injury as anyone in pain would. Moe only allowed me to work the areas he chose. His quick snips towards my hands guided my strokes.

We were not making much progress; the places I needed to work were exactly the places he would not allow me to touch. At the beginning of each session, I had to re-gain Moe's trust, "Please let me help." He would surrender to my touch, only a bit and resentfully, until I pushed his boundaries. In the "approved areas", I rubbed and worked until he was relaxed and actually enjoying himself. Then, I would attempt to sneak in some light strokes to the hypertonic muscles in the "unapproved areas". At which point, the massage would abruptly end with him removing himself from the table.

His growing aggravation with me and my attempts to release his muscles were evidence that this method would never work. As a therapist, I knew we were never going to get anywhere if this power struggle continued. As Moe's friend, I knew he just was not prepared to let me in. I gave up.

After the failed attempts at therapeutic massage on the table, our only option for muscle manipulation was when he decided I could pet, not massage, him and only where he liked it. Occasionally, I tried to sneak relief into his hip muscles. That was always when he would make his exits. His will was stronger than mine own.

Since working on his physical body was not allowed, I thought we might have better luck if we worked on Moe's emotional, mental and spiritual bodies instead. This is where the root cause of disease is after all and I could channel off pain while I was in there.

My friend was always so irritated at the announcement of another session. Afraid that I would hurt him, he permitted only a hands off approach. I began by just looking at him. He made himself comfortable but was still on guard.

Our first energy session uncovered a surprising revelation about my friend. As I scanned his energy field, the area above his front paws blinked white flashes of light. "What's this?" I asked.

Moe crossed one paw over the other.

Gently uncrossing them, I looked closer and held my concentration. Next, a wave of emotion slammed me. There was anger and loss there. I caressed the soft pads of his feet. After feeling as much as I could, I developed an understanding of what he was hiding in this part of his energy field. He missed his claws and was furious that they were taken from him. I had not thought about this in years; I guess I assumed he had just accepted it. He had not. It had been ten years since they were taken from him and he was still fuming. My friend had long been waiting to express his feelings about this to me.

There was a myriad of emotion swimming in the end of his paws. He felt violated. He was ashamed; in losing his claws, he had lost pride. His claws were once a source of power for him. Now the empty knuckles were a source of dishonor. He moved them away from me again, folding them under his body. His fear of vets or any other person who sought to manipulate his body with or without his permission was valid. After that, how could he trust anyone?

I fought to keep my tears from washing away my focus. "I'm sorry sweetie. I didn't know they were going to do that to you."

While I was away at college, my parents had Moe de-clawed. They disregarded my wishes for him and had the procedure done when I could do nothing to stop it.

"You know I didn't want that for you, don't you?" He was waiting for that apology, it didn't matter to him who was responsible. He just needed to hear it.

Moe said nothing. He closed his big green eyes and allowed me to stroke his toes. An energy release came from his center. He sighed and began purring. He had released only what he was willing to. Forgiveness, sometimes, can only be granted in small doses. Kissing my friend on his head, I ended our session and left him to nap on the table.

As, I left the room, I kept repeating to myself, "I never knew." The implications of what I had just found were thick with revelation. Of course he was pissed; he should have been. He was traumatized by surgery and awoke to find something precious was taken from him.

There is no dignity for a cat without claws. I was never a proponent for de-clawing because I felt it was cruel. Now I understood it from Moe's perspective. It absolutely was a violation of his personal power. Firstly, it was done without any regard for his best interest. Secondly, it was done without his permission. That is the very definition of violation. It was his body; therefore, he should have control over it. Thirdly, for a cat, claws are power.

They use them to hunt and fight. They use them to tear flesh and torture prey. Claws are a cat's very means of survival. His claws were gone; he considered that nothing less than a dethroning.

Moe's de-clawing should never have been allowed to happen. I hoped, by forgiving my parents and me, he had regained some of his personal power. After all, that is what forgiveness does.

Moe's pure white paws were one of my favorite places to touch. The pads were painted with pink and gray. I enjoyed pondering the markings. In the past, when I tried to rub them, he would always move them away from me. Now I knew why. After our session that day, he granted me permission to touch them again. Moe never fully recovered his power, nor did he ever completely forgive the incident. All that could be done was done; his claws could not be given back. An apology was all I could give to make things right. His acceptance was conditioned with remorse, much like my delivery. Paw rubs became part of our regular petting routine. I took great pleasure in rounding each toe with my fingers. It was wonderful to see him enjoy it. Small though it was, we had our first success with energy healing.

Even though I understood his disdain for the medical profession, I continued to take Moe to new vets to see if they could help with the incontinence. Their lack of clarity on the issue was astounding. Not one realized the incontinence was a result of the spinal injury. When the office visits concluded, I would leave without a word. If they could not figure that out, then they were not the doctor for us.

Moe and I kept working and talking together. My intention was always to heal his back and restore spinal organization. He had other intentions. Like the loss of claws, he had endured other traumas over the years. During another energy session, I was again surprised at what was uncovered. I scanned his body, listening and looking for what he would express to me. There was something, almost imperceptible, in his heart chakra. Patiently, I waited for the story to unfold. Before long, in my mind's eye, a picture appeared. There was a hole in his heart. It jostled me. Steadying my focus, I felt, looked and listened for more. From the fuzz and haze of my mind's eye, the picture became more clear. It was our beloved Heather Feather. He was still grieving and missing her after all those years. Intense waves of grief flooded my senses. I empathized with my boy; he really did love her. His heart was expressing pain from long ago. This was his chance to release it, in the company of compassion. When the waves of grief ceased to flow from him, my hands and heart opened into full channel. I funneled the comfort that can only come from God and the Angels into his heart. I held my hands above his heart chakra until the hole was near closed. Moe let out a sigh. Neither of us said a word; there was nothing to say. I finished channeling into and balancing out the rest of his main chakras and let him rest on the table in the peace our session had created for him.

Afterwards, I thought about the old expression describing the pain from death and loss as a hole in the heart. Until then, I had never found an actual hole. Until then, it was only a euphemism. Heather had been gone for about fourteen years. That entire time, Moe had held an empty space for her. This set my mind into motion; animals experience grief and loss just as humans do. I knew this from watching Moe when we first lost our Heather.

Until I touched the hole she left, I did not understand the extent to which he was grieving her loss. His grief was stuck in his energy field, waiting for a safe space and a consoling a friend, before it could be released. Despite all the time I had shared with my friend, I was unaware of the sadness he was carrying. The hole in his heart was not fully closed; would it ever be? After fourteen years, he still needed to let loose with a good long cry. If I had known how he felt, I would have supported and comforted him when she first went missing. As it happened, I do not think I ever even said a word to him. He had suffered the devastation of her loss alone.

A completely new picture was now forming for me. My perception of the friend by side was changing. In our first years together, I had grossly underestimated him. In fact, I did not really know him. Though I loved him dearly, I had only loved him as a pet. Now I was venturing on making acquaintance with his true spirit. Hearing him speak had been enough to keep me shallowly amused before. What we were now embarking upon was a profound discovery. The rich spectrum of emotions, from which he colored his life, was as intensely colored as mine. Our energy work had uncovered his anger, his fear and his grief. Our conversations and shared intimacy had uncovered joy and sorrow. I longed to comfort him, heal him, relieve him of any pain and do my best to bring him peace. Mostly, I desired to understand him and be his friend, not his "owner".

King

Occasionally, Moe reminded me that I did not, in fact, own him. Once we had a conversation in which he relayed his perspective on who he really was. He started by complaining that I called him my baby. "I am not your baby. You are not my mother", his voice was cold and irritated.

"I know I'm not your mother." I was hurt by his words.

"Don't call me a baby. I am not a baby. You don't own me either you know", his tone was growing even more spiteful.

"I'm sorry." My heart was wounded, where was this was coming from? We were just lying on the couch relaxing. Why was he bringing this up?

"Moe, these are just things I say. I don't really mean them."

Those phrases were adopted without much thought or attachment to their meaning. It had never occurred to me before that Moe would find my terms of endearment offensive and demeaning. His admonishment conveyed his point; owning another living thing was a preposterous notion and he was a liberated soul of his own free will.

I never meant to own him however; my intent was lost in translation. As I reflected on his annoyance, I concluded that pet "ownership" is a ridiculous notion. Referring to our relationship with that term was an insult to his spirit.

I asked, "What would you call it then? What is this arrangement we have?"

His tone much softer this time, Moe responded wisely, "We are your guardians. You are our keepers."

"Okay buddy. I am sorry. That sounds much better, much more respectful. I won't call you my baby anymore."

Moe gestured with his eyes, blinking slowly. His point was made and he was content again. He drifted off on my lap.

As his little motor ran, I thought about what he said. It really was a much more appropriate way to describe our relationship. Looking back on all the years, I realized he was my guardian. He deserved respect and recognition for all he had done for me. He was always concerned with my highest good. He was always in tune with my feelings and definitely made me aware when he did not approve of friends or boyfriends. He comforted me when I was down and celebrated life's joys right there with me. He probably knew me better than I knew myself. Just like a parent, he loved me unconditionally and watched me grow. Moe endured my variable successes and failures as a best friend would. He was the one I came home to. We shared it all, even if I could not perceive how much we were actually sharing. He was right; he was not a baby and I did not own him.

Moe was my guardian. It was a noble title he deserved. He had more than earned it. He was a Saint for putting up with my ignorance for all those years. I had a new level of respect for my friend; keeping him was an honor and a privilege.

Being reprimanded for my inappropriate baby talk had me feeling like a failure. It was a feeling I was becoming used to. We had very few successes regarding Moe's healing. The more we talked, the more I found out how I had screwed up at being his keeper. He was upset about so many things: his claws, Heather and my past ignorance of his feelings. We had not found another chiropractor and there still was no veterinarian to help us. No progress in healing his spine, nerves and muscles was made. The gravity of our situation was pulling me down. The more I worried, the more pressure I put on myself. All of that pressure caused me to move in and out of denial. Moe no longer had any control over his bladder and now he had losing control of his bowels. He lived every day in pain. My faith was faltering. We needed a success.

On top of everything, Moe was developing cataracts. The last thing we needed was another health problem. There was no way I was going to let my boy go blind. That would just be too much suffering. There was no point in it. Enough was enough.

Healing Moe's sight became my most important ambition. A common treatment for kidney stones is to use sound waves from ultrasound machines to break them up into smaller pieces so they can be comfortably passed. I reasoned that if urologists could use sound energy to break up stones, then I could use light energy for a very similar application.

For weeks, I had been working on my theory. I tried often but could never find the right circumstances or create the right conditions. Moe was often annoyed with me for accessing his energy and using crystals to laser light energy into his eyes. He complained that I was too invasive and often refused me.

On a whim, one afternoon, I decided to try again. Determined to fix his vision, I dug my heels in, and then projected my thoughts out to the heavens: "There is no possibility that this cat will lose his sight, there is no need for this. I will not allow it. It will not happen." I was rooted in my thoughts. My emotions were rock solid. Everything in me had spontaneously aligned. I had the will to make it happen. This time I would find the exact vibration that would break up the filmy deposits in my beloved's eyes.

Moe was annoyed, as usual, when I approached him with my crystals. He stirred from his position on the chair. "What now? What are you going to do?"

"Let's see if we can get those cataracts gone," I said.

During all of my prior attempts, he had no idea why I was pointing the stones into his eyes. I realized I had neglected to tell him what I was attempting. He had never given me permission to do work on him.

"Moe, it's the milky stuff in your eyeballs. Can you see well?"

The cataracts were in the very first stages. His sight was probably only beginning to fail. He said nothing and relaxed for me.

Then, I heard another, different voice tell him, "Let her do this."

Too immersed in the moment to question who that voice was, I went ahead with my focused intention. The prayers that fell from my lips pleaded for the perfect vibration to heal his eyes. My crown chakra opened and I my body began to buzz. The energy, that was filling me, was then enough to flow out through my hands and into the crystals, which amplified and directed it.

After just a few seconds, pulsations of light energy reached inside Moe's right eye. I had done something different this time. Maybe it was gaining his permission. Maybe I had more focus than I did during my earlier attempts. Maybe it was both of those things. Maybe the strange, new voice I heard was someone who was helping us. Whatever it was, I had no time to question it. I held my space and intention. With the symbolic sight of my mind's eye, I witnessed the cataract breaking up and dissolving. My heart beat fast at the marvelous sight. Could I hold on long enough to do the other eye?

Silencing the fear of failure, I dug my heels in deeper. When the pulsing energy stopped, I moved to his other eye to start again. Miraculously, the energy began to pulse once more. Moe was peaceful and receptive. We were having a winning moment.

Only minutes later, my body stopped buzzing and the energy flowing from my hands faded. It was done. With some pressure off of my shoulders, I kissed my friend on his head and thanked him for letting me help him. He nodded off unceremoniously.

Over the next few days, I watched his eyes optimistically for signs of improvement. Slowly, the white milky coating retreated. After a week, there was only a tiny speck left in the center of his pupils. The cataracts were gone. Moe was delighted. This tiny success renewed my faith and strength. I was going to keep plugging away at this thing hanging over us. Moe would be healed.

The apartment we were living in offered neither of us the country life we desired. The energy of our home was increasingly depressing. Our stress was sticking to the walls. It was time to move again. Getting away from the scene of the fall might help us both lift our spirits. I also hoped that if I gave my sweetheart a backyard and some places to explore he would get some much-needed exercise and stimulation. We moved out to a little cottage in the foothills just northwest of town.

During the move, my dad phoned to tell me my grandmother, his mom, had suddenly passed away. There was no way I could make it back to Michigan for her funeral. Financially, I was busted. The moving expenses had just eaten my very last penny. I regretfully informed my father I just was not going to make it. Moe was sick and I was the only one who could care for him. Leaving him was not an option.

My father responded peacefully, "Its okay Kerry".

I pushed and powered through the move, all the while feeling like nothing was okay. My stress was mounting. The guilt I felt over missing my grandma's funeral added weight to the cross that I bore.

After all of my things were in our new home, I made the last trip back to the old apartment to get Moe, his food and his food dish, the same way I had done so many times before. As we drove, I excitedly told him how lovely our new place was. It had a big yard that backed up to the mountains. It was alive with birds, bugs, and fresh air. I carried him from the car, through the walkway, to the side door. Instead of taking him inside right away, I carried him around the perimeter of the property, showing him the back and side yards. As always, I made sure he noted the place where our yard met the road and reminded him about cars. He was enjoying the sights and sounds of his new surroundings. Our last apartment was so boring, completely devoid of nature. His ears flicked excitedly. I also reminded him of dangers such as bears, snakes, owls, coyotes, foxes and other predatory animals. He would not be the only hunter stalking our new property.

Certain he was now aware of all-important outdoor boundaries, I carefully placed him just inside the side door of our new home. He made the usual inspection. His eyes were wide and his ears were alert. His tail was attempting to go up. I unpacked as he sniffed every corner. He found his food and had a bite. Looking up from the food bowl, he casually asked, "Where's the bed?"

"We don't have one anymore. The old one was a real piece of junk. It was hurting my back. We can use the futon mattress until we get another."

He squinted his eyes with distaste, "Oh."

"Sorry buddy. What do you think though? Do you like our new place?"

"It's nice", he replied as he walked off to find a place to nap.

So much for a detailed commentary, I thought to myself. Optimistic about our new home, I wanted to hear more; that it was just the best house ever and that he loved it. Oh well, I guess cats find no use in sugarcoated small talk.

Our new place was working out nicely. Moe began taking daily patrols around the property. We loved being in the country again. About a week after we had settled in, a friend stopped by to see the new place. I gave him the grand tour. We came full circle back into the kitchen, where there were drops of blood all over the floor. They had not been there a minute ago.

"Where is all this blood coming from?" I looked over at Moe; he was sitting in front of the door. Thinking he was cut, I searched him for any kind of wound. There were no apparent injuries.

Now completely confused, I asked, "What is going on?"

My friend painfully pointed to Moe, "I think it's coming from his... um... ahem... you know."

"What? Tell me!"

My friend awkwardly pointed at Moe, "His penis."

I shrieked, "Oh my God!"

He was right. It was. My heart was racing with panic. What the hell was happening? What should I do? It was Sunday. All of the animal hospitals were closed for the weekend. Where would I take him?

Moe was not even aware he was bleeding. He gave me no indication that he was in pain; in fact, he seemed quite contented. I frantically looked through the phonebook and found the only veterinary office open. They told me to bring him in right away.

We drove way above the legal speed limit to get to the emergency hospital. My anxiety was now affecting Moe and he realized he was on his way to the vet. His contentment completely vanished as he heard me explain his symptoms to the receptionist. She assured me it would not be long and we took our seats in the waiting room. Moe was wrapped in a towel, in my lap. We sat, waited and prayed.

The doctor preformed an exam and consulted with her superior. We were at the Colorado State University hospital. It was outfitted with every latest veterinary innovation. Moe was fitted with an IV and catheter. The doctors requested to keep him overnight for observation.

Moe did not want to stay. His eyes were wide with anxiety. He did not like the invasive procedures or doctors and technicians performing them. He shot me a fearful glance when he heard their request to keep him. I secretly assured him that he would be fine; we needed to find out what was wrong.

My heart was heavy with worry, full of apprehension and fear. Though it was difficult to leave him, I played tough, like a mother who is strong for her child. I kissed him and scratched his ears lovingly, then closed the door behind me. Fearful tears stained my face; what was wrong, what did he need, would he be all right?

First thing the next morning, I called to check on him. The receptionist informed me that Moe had an infection and they needed to do an expensive ultrasound. The cost of the test now added to my long list of worries. If it was just an infection, couldn't he come home with antibiotics? Moe was scared and alone, he did not need to stay there any longer than was absolutely necessary.

We were struggling financially as it was. Outrageous bills from a university hospital would push me further into the red. I weighed Moe's healthcare needs against the cost of providing them to him. It was a consideration no one should ever have to make. I assumed an infection could clear up easily, it was time to take him home.

When I showed up to retrieve my sweetheart, it was clear that the receptionist was not expecting me. I insisted that I see Moe and his doctor.

The doctor, also surprised by my arrival, informed me that she would not release Moe. She asked me if I had misunderstood, "I'm not sure you understand, Kerry. We need to do an ultrasound to check his bladder and kidneys."

I spoke genuinely to the doctor, "Is this ultrasound absolutely necessary? I am worried about the costs. Wouldn't normal blood and lab work find what we are looking for? I understand your caution. If his kidneys are infected, we need to treat aggressively. However, can't we just see if the antibiotics clear this up before we go on to order very expensive tests?"

In an attempt to gain even more of her sympathy, I also explained that I had been surviving on only potatoes for the last week and there was no gas in my car. She kindly agreed to send us home with very strong antibiotics and explicit orders to take them all as directed.

As I left the exam room, doubts about my ability to pay the bill crept over me. The hospital would not release my kitty until the bill was settled. Thankfully, I was approved for a line of credit. We had racked up over six hundred dollars in less than twenty-four hours of care.

In spite of my worry over finances, I resolved to enjoy Moe's homecoming. Nothing could steal away my relief, Moe was going to be okay and somehow our bills would be paid.

This last, very scary experience demonstrated that it was absolutely imperative that we find a good vet. We could not afford more emergencies, financially or emotionally. He needed someone who completely understood his situation. We needed a compassionate, intelligent veterinarian who truly cared and could offer an affordable treatment plan.

We found what we needed through my friend Lizz. She and I had known each other for a few years but rarely had opportunities to spend time together. As luck, or divine intervention would have it, she had just started working as a veterinary technician again. She had formerly given up on her career because she could no longer work for corrupt, uncaring and money driven doctors. Recently, she had found a wonderful doctor and was now working for him in his clinic. She encouraged me to take Moe to see him.

In the past Lizz had done marvelous things for animals; I had listened eagerly to all of her amazing stories. Her life's purpose was in service to all animals and I trusted her dear love for them. I made us an appointment for the next week.

Still skeptical, I drove Moe to his appointment. No other doctors we had seen were able to understand Moe's very specific case. Beyond Lizz's recommendation, there was no cause to believe this doctor would be any different. We had left quite a few offices in despair. Of course, once again, Moe was not happy to be visiting any kind of clinic.

"Stop worrying," I told him, "I'm not going to let anything bad happen to you." My words did nothing to console him.

Dr. S was immediately likeable. His presence was personable, not stuffy. He wore jeans and a flannel, not a cold, bleached, white lab coat. He smiled a lot and seemed to be genuinely concerned for Moe's wellbeing. His eyes gave him away as an animal lover. They looked directly into mine as he carefully listened to Moe's complete medical history. It was the first time any professional had given us uninterrupted and concentrated attention.

When I was finished telling our story, our new doctor responded, "Okay. So the urinary incontinence is secondary to the initial injury."

Eureka! I was thrilled. He actually understood!

Excitedly I answered, "Yes. The fall caused it all. The nerves surrounding the dislocated vertebrae are connected to the bladder and bowels. They are not functioning. Now what can we do about it?"

Dr. S's eyes grew sad; he cocked his head to the side and said, "Unfortunately, there's not much we can do."

My excitement of finally finding the right doctor fell right through my shoes.

"There must be something?" I pleaded.

He was palpating Moe as we spoke. Dr. S manually emptied his bladder and explained that Moe was unable to empty it completely on his own.

"The bladder is like a balloon," Dr. S spoke sympathetically, "it stretches to hold increasing amounts of fluid. His infection is cleared up temporarily but he will be in constant risk of others. I need time to think about a treatment plan."

Dr. S's manner and insights were respectable. His compassion was unmistakable. I was relieved that we had our new vet. Unfortunately, my relief was short-lived due to everything else I had learned that day. My distress over Moe was growing, my emotions were becoming erratic. Things were getting worse. We had already been through so many ups and downs. It seemed, with every victory, came a defeat. It was imperative to keep my head in order to provide Moe with the care he needed; I could not allow myself to lose control. We pressed on.

Our new home provided us with an extra bedroom. It was perfect for a massage and healing space. The little money that came in from seeing new clients was a blessing. Moe and I spent a lot of time in there attempting great healings. We worked often and found little relief. With every session, I held on to my faith in the power of God and miracles. Every session was a chance for a miracle and profound healing. We focused on realigning his spine and regenerating nerves and soft tissue. We were able to release a lot of pain. Other than that, I was not very effective in achieving my intentions. Despite our many efforts, things were not improving.

Lizz came for a visit again. We discussed how excellent Dr. S was. We concluded that he was a superior veterinarian based on his compassion for and understanding of Moe's condition. We labored over Dr. S's insights about Moe as we watched him dribble pee on the concrete. Eventually, Moe would not be able to pee at all. The nerves were in atrophy. Lizz suggested that I take him in again to see if Dr. S had thought long enough to discover a treatment plan.

In the next few days, we did just that. Dr. S greeted us happily with another genuine smile. He expressed Moe's overfilled bladder again. Our good doctor warned that if Moe's bladder got too full, it could burst. That would be an extremely painful death.

Dr. S had formed a plan. Because it was not efficient, economically or physically, to bring Moe in every time he needed to pee, Lizz would teach me to manually express his bladder. If I could learn to do so, it would then be possible for me to manage Moe's care.

Lizz was so helpful and patient with my instruction. Moe was not helpful or patient. He soon learned that the sight of Lizz meant I would be squeezing and pulling on him again. He thought it best to hide every time he saw her.

Learning to express a bladder proved to be very difficult. Moe struggled with me. My first attempts were awkward and clumsy; many times he walked away angry and tender. He once scolded me after another failed attempt, "You are always doing that now."

"I'm trying to help you. We need this." My response to his scolding was stubborn and strong. On this issue, I would not waver.

At first, it was impossible to even locate his bladder. Lizz patiently instructed me to feel for a balloon. When I found it, a squeeze with just the right angle and pressure would expel the contents.

Finally, after four days of no peeing and no success, Moe's bladder was enlarged enough that I could not miss it. Gently but firmly I applied the right squeeze and out came the pee. Moe shot me a sideways glance with a stunned and confused expression. I suppose peeing when you hadn't intended to would be quite a shock.

I giggled happily, "See buddy, I have been trying to help you. It worked! We can empty your bladder now."

Moe looked back at me with humble eyes. I paid no attention to his embarrassment. This was a victory we should celebrate. This meant that Dr. S's treatment plan would work. Moe would be safe in my care.

As the weeks went by, Moe and I were slowly becoming overwhelmed with our roles of patient and caregiver. We found less and less time to just love each other. Neither of us were happy. Moe was always in pain. I could never leave him for more than a few hours at a time; we couldn't risk his bladder becoming too full.

When I did get away for a few hours, I allowed myself complete denial of the entire situation. Afterwards, I would return home to find my love resting on a pee-soaked towel, stinking of neglect. Heartbroken and guilt ridden, I dutifully removed the towels and cleaned up my friend. Moe's health was becoming even worse due to his body's increasing stiffness. He could no longer clean himself and was getting bladder infections more and more often.

We continued on this way for a few months. I was helping him as best as I could, refusing to let go of hope. Occasionally, I remembered my role as his friend as he climbed on my belly for some rubbing. There was still comfort in the sound of his little motor running. His purring had a way of putting me in a blissful state.

Dr. S had given us some cream to protect Moe's skin from urine scald. When applied correctly, it was effective and I was able to leave my friend for a few hours. The instructions were simple enough, however the stress of caring for Moe was beginning to get the better of me. My priorities were all mixed up. More of my time was spent blowing off steam with friends than taking vigilant care of Moe. Instead of inspecting and caring for all of Moe's parts diligently at each application, I applied the cream hastily and rushed out the door. Each time I left, my routine went something like this: express the bladder, apply cream, provide a fresh towel to sleep on, pile on my denial and race off for some extracurricular nonsense. My behavior was terribly irresponsible.

One morning, after a week of that routine, a voice awakened me, "Kerry, don't be so afraid that Moe will die."

My Angel repeated himself three times as I arose to full awareness. It was a warning I couldn't understand. I was not worried Moe would die; I expected him to make a full recovery. Why would my Angel tell me that?

With those words pushed from my rational mind, I went on with my morning. Moe and I snuggled for a bit and then went outside to express his bladder. That morning his bladder was elusive; it couldn't be located. This was day four of no pee. With the words of my Angel haunting me, I decided that we should do some work before I left for the day.

This time, I began the session by asking Moe what he wanted. He replied as if he was grinding his teeth, "I want to peeeeeee!"

"Okay, let's take care of it." I began to channel into his small body and chakras. He was more annoyed than ever, making repeated attempts to escape the table. Tired and frustrated, I finally allowed his escape. At the end of the session, it was apparent that I was missing something. I asked God to show me what that was; I asked to feel what Moe was feeling.

As the day unfolded, the events of the morning were forgotten. On the drive to a part-time job, a sudden, stinging, stabbing pain shot through my pants. The intensity had me howling as I parked my car. Unable to bear the pain, I screamed, "What the hell is this?"

Later that evening, Lizz stopped by to check Moe. We had planned to give him some IV fluids because he had not been drinking. As I spoke with Lizz about Moe, the days events unfolded in my mind and it gradually dawned on me that Moe was in danger.

I understood it all in an instant, the Angel's warning, Moe's request to pee, my request to feel what Moe was feeling and the pain I felt. It all finally sunk in.

"Lizz, before we give him fluids please check his bladder. I haven't been able to express it in four days." Her face grew grim. She checked and found it was dangerously full. Her expression changed to alarm. "He's going to burst."

Fear tempted me to move into panic. The words I heard my Angel speak held me steady. "Don't be so afraid," echoed in my mind. I spoke calmly to Lizz,

"We can't let fear take us."

She looked at me as if I was a foolish lunatic. "Kerry, this is an awful way to die! We have to get him somewhere!" It was late. Again, all the clinics were closed.

Lizz moved into action. She was either motivated by my words, or by my certain insanity. Her purpose took over as she began inspecting my kitty and asking questions. I am not proud of what she found.

The cream I was applying every day was caked to a crust. It was preventing any urine from exiting. I admitted to her what an idiot I was. She smiled with compassion for me as we prepared a bath for Moe in the kitchen sink. She soaked him and gently scrubbed away as much of the caked-on crust as she could. She spent at least an hour soaking and scrubbing Moe all the while struggling to keep him in the sink.

When we pulled Moe from the water to check for any progress, his penis was still not completely clean. Lizz checked his bladder again. She spoke in astonishment, "It's not as full!"

"Check again," I said, "there's no way."

"Really, it's not as full. He could not have peed. He is still crusted over. What just happened?"

"It's a miracle," I beamed.

Lizz smiled and continued to look for logic and reason.

I continued, "It's a miracle you even came over today. I would have gone on as if everything was just fine. Meanwhile Moe was about die, painfully. I am an idiot, Lizz. You just saved his life!" Disgusted with myself and eternally grateful to Lizz, I had never felt so stupid and so thankful at the same time.

Lizz was still very concerned for Moe's life. "Kerry, you need to take Moe to an emergency hospital."

"It's almost 11:00 p.m., can't we make it until morning? Do you think he will burst?"

Lizz's answer was only a little reassuring, "His bladder isn't as full, but it is still risky."

Though I was frightened, I made the decision to wait for Dr. S, based on my Angels warning. It was a gamble if he would make it until morning.

That night, we flirted with death. The very little sleep I managed to get was laced with nightmares. At six a.m., my eyes opened. The menacing danger was tangible, it hung in the air above us. Dr. S's clinic did not open until eight. We still had so long to go. Carefully, I lifted Moe and placed him on my chest. He winced. I began to pray and meditate as I had done so many other times before. It was all I knew to do. We were making our way to God, just as we had done after his fall. I channeled as best as I could, desperately shutting out the fear and pushing away the hand of death. We climbed out through my crown chakra until I sensed a powerful and divine presence.

I cried to God showing Him my kitty. "Help us, please. We need a miracle!" His answer was shocking.

"I have already given you a miracle." The voice was indescribably powerful and penetrating. I wasn't expecting it. Lizz's face flashed through my mind's eye.

"I know," I said "but he's going to burst. Please, we need another."

No words came in response. Nothing happened, I just laid there with Moe, waiting. We still had an hour before the clinic would open.

A moment later a voice spoke to me, "Kerry, take Moe now."

I jerked up from wherever I was. The clock read seven thirty a.m. Time had moved but I had not perceived its passing. Stunned, I wondered aloud, "what just happened?" An hour had just passed in only a minute.

I got dressed and brushed my teeth in a flash. We quickly loaded up and rushed to see Dr. S.

On the short drive to the clinic, I processed what God had told me. Lizz really had delivered us a miracle. She really had saved Moe's life. In the early hours of that morning, God showed me her face and recalled the miracle that he had given me through her. She had been his vessel and her actions had spared my sweetheart. I was overcome with gratitude.

Dr. S just happened to be in early that morning. We arrived at seven forty-five a.m. Immediately, he took Moe and me into the back room. He examined Moe. His face spoke volumes. He was disgusted, both by what he found and with me. Dr. S felt Moe's bladder. With unstated urgency, he asked me to leave Moe in his care. He would start a catheter and keep him for a few days. Unbelievably grateful that we had arrived safely into the hands of Dr. S, I just knew Moe would make it. We had just experienced a miracle. I had come terribly close to losing my best friend and my denial and neglect were the cause. Incredibly ashamed, I hid my eyes from our trusted doctor and stared at the floor. It was clear I needed a few days of relief as a caretaker. Overwhelmed by our situation, I no longer had any good sense.

I whispered to my brave friend, "I'll be back to get you soon." As I left the clinic, my ashamed eyes poured tears of grief and exhaustion.

Later in the day, I went back to the clinic to check on Moe. Dr. S and Lizz were able to clear away the mess and get Moe catheterized. My poor kitty looked so tired, he was miserable but hanging on. Dr. S planned to allow the catheter to clear Moe's bladder completely. Though I didn't want to leave him, I apologized to my friend again and left for the night.

The next morning was a Friday. As soon as I woke, I drove to the clinic to see my boy. Moe was sitting up, licking his paws when I walked in. "Moe! You look so good!"

He looked up surprised to hear my voice. I opened the door to the cage where he was resting to pet him. Moe's incredibly improved condition was unbelievable. He was purring, his fur was clean and fluffy and his eyes had restored vigor. His strength had returned and he was relieved to be feeling good again. I was not expecting such a quick recovery: he was better than he had been in a long time.

The doc came back into the room. My heart swelled with gratitude as he entered. "He looks so good. I can't believe it!"

Dr. S smiled and explained that he wanted Moe to stay the weekend. Dr. S thought it was best to leave the catheter in until Moe's system was completely flushed.

"But he will be all alone," I pleaded.

There would be no one there all weekend except for a few visits by staff each day for feedings, administering medication and bedding changes.

"Wouldn't he be better off at home with me. I can monitor him constantly. He is doing so well and as long as that catheter stays in, we are golden."

"Kerry, he might pull out the catheter," Dr. S warned.

Dr. S was not aware of my ability to communicate with Moe. Silently, I assured myself it would all be okay if Moe and I had a talk later. If I explained everything, he would understand not to pull the catheter out. Moe would listen; he would do as I asked.

"Dr. S we can do this. I will make sure he doesn't pull it out. Please, I can't bear to leave him all alone. I'll bring him back on Monday. He is the love of my life!"

Dr. S. was convinced that Moe would pull the catheter out. He gave me his home number and told me to call right away if he did. Overjoyed and overcome I thanked Dr S with a hug. He was a blessing.

When Moe and I arrived home, I warned him not to pull out the catheter. I explained that he needed it, even though it was so uncomfortable.

"It's helping you pee," I said. Moe completely ignored me, he had no interest in any discussion. He continued with his purring and grooming, happy to feel so good.

There was no point continuing a one sided conversation; I relinquished. Maybe we both just needed to rest. I made a cozy bed with blankets and a laundry basket and set it in front of the heater vent. Inside, I placed my friend with his food and water. When he was comfortable, I collapsed into bed. Thanking God one more time, I drifted into a deep sleep.

First thing the next morning, I discovered Moe had pulled out the catheter, just like Dr. S said he would. "Moe! I told you not to do that! Why did you do that?"

He looked at me without a care, "I couldn't take it anymore."

"You shouldn't have done that and you know it." My words were sharp.

Panicked that he had hurt himself, I searched his bed for the small pieces of plastic tubing.

"Moe you butt-head! What if there are pieces stuck inside you?"

Immediately, I called our beloved Dr. S. Not surprised at all to hear what Moe had done, he invited us down to the clinic right away.

Dr. S calmly examined my stubborn friend. He assured me that everything was fine. The catheter had been in long enough to do its job and there were no missing pieces. Moe's bladder was completely empty, a condition he had not felt in months.

Dr. S continued on to give me a thorough education in male kitty anatomy. He lectured me on the importance of keeping Moe clean. Then he suggested we switch from cream to petroleum jelly and made me apply it in front of him.

"I'm sorry Dr. S, I have totally lost my head. I know this was all my fault." Still embarrassed and ashamed, I endured the lesson.

Making no comment on my stupidity and apparent neglect, Dr S. showed me our recent lab results. They indicated the exact bacteria that were causing Moe's current infection. "How are you with needles? This infection is only treatable by injection."

Eager to regain my role as Moe's caretaker and protector, I answered bravely, "I can do it."

Dr. S. then spent more of his free time teaching me how to inject my kitty with a syringe. Once he was certain I could manage, he loaded us up with enough antibiotic and syringes and sent us on our way. With my fear of needles now abated, I thanked Dr. S. again, knowing I could never express how grateful I really was.

As we drove home, I once more thanked God, this time for both Lizz and Dr. S. They were so kind and compassionate and delivered professional yet loving care to Moe. Their genuine concern for him had saved his life. Other clinics or doctors would have charged us so much more and given us so much less. Dr. S and Lizz had successfully taught me the skills I needed to care for Moe, thus avoiding costly daily clinic visits. However, we also needed lab work, clinic stays, x-rays, catheters and a myriad of antibiotics. All of this had cost me less than three-hundred dollars at Dr. S's small clinic. His office never pressured me to pay, I paid when I could. It was obvious to me that Dr. S cared for the animals in his clinic as if they were his own. What he did for us was motivated by love, not money. Dr. S. and Lizz were a great team who kept the best interests of the animals a priority above anything else. I knew no other doctor or veterinary technician who would even consider taking time from his or her days off to help an animal. Their actions and quality of care spoke volumes about the content of their hearts. As I thanked God for them, I wished other doctors and technicians would take inspiration from them.

Administering the daily shots was almost as painful for me as it was for Moe. His neck was getting tough and sore from repeated poking. With each nervous injection came the fear that I would hurt him. A few times, I caught muscle under the needle and Moe just about jumped out of his skin. Despite the difficulty, we never missed a dose.

Ten days later, we had finished all of the medicine. Moe's infection was completely cleared. He was better again and I had overcome my fear of needles. We had ourselves another, small victory.

After this last terrible scare, after almost losing my friend due to my irresponsible stupidity, I became extra diligent about hygiene and care. Moe was never left alone too long and we increased our efforts to keep his urinary tract in good health by mixing supplements in with his breakfast. We were supplementing so much in fact, his breakfast dish had more powdery pill in it than it did food. Moe was taking cranberry, arginex and glucosamine chondroitin. I was taking attitude and dirty looks. Most mornings, he would sniff his dish, shoot me a nasty look and just walk away. No matter how much I emphasized his need to eat it, he rarely complied. For Moe, taste negated necessity.

During all of this time, our conversations were progressing nicely. His voice was stronger and clearer in my head. He had been waiting his whole life to speak with me. At some point during his adolescence, he came to understand that I would hear him someday. He never told me how knew, just that he had been waiting a long time. That time was finally here, our dialogue now had a genuine flow. Even when I wasn't near him, I could tune in to him and ask how things were. My gifts had finally opened enough for our connection to be strong; there were no more glitches on my end of the line.

Perhaps his Guides and Angels showed him we would talk one day. Occasionally, I heard them counseling him. Hearing those conversations was difficult; they were private and were held at a very high frequency. The whispers I did catch were insightful, directive and loving, just like the whispers of my own Guides and Angels. Perhaps, long ago they whispered to him that I would "wake up" one day. Perhaps, they inspired him with something to look forward to; it filled me with sorrow and regret that he waited almost his entire life for me to clear my end of the line.

Our healing sessions on the massage table were not working. Moe was increasingly uncomfortable with the table and afraid that I would hurt him. His pain was intensifying, and so was his frustration with me poking around in his energy field. We needed a different approach.

An idea came to me in meditation one evening. In the middle of the night, I awoke with terrible back pain accompanied by a strong feeling that I should use the kundalini breathing method. This technique was fairly new to me; throughout the past few years, I was working with it periodically to clear blockages from my own spine and chakras. At times, I did achieve levels of higher awareness and successfully removed blockages for myself.

With all my energies so focused on bringing healing to Moe, I didn't get a chance to practice kundalini often. That evening, there was a gentle nudge to use it. With the pain in my back and a push from spirit to motivate me, I began breathing and chanting.

In the past, my chanting always followed the dogmatic teachings from the books I had read. I never deviated by changing words or technique. This time I began the same way I had before, "So… Hum… So… Hum… So… Hum." The chant was graceful. The words were easy to remember and their meaning resonated, "I am peace."

After only a few breaths, a voice instructed me, "Je-Sus."

"Huh?" I thought. Kundalini is an eastern form of prayer and meditation; Jesus has nothing to do with it. The idea was preposterous. I continued with "So… Hum."

"Je-Sus!" The voice spoke again, this time louder.

"What the hell," I thought, laughing at my own choice of words, "I better listen."

"Je-in breath, Sus-out breath." "Je-Sus, Je-sus, Je-sus." I had no idea what I was doing. It was difficult to ignore the questions my chattery mind was forming. "Je-sus, Je-sus, Je-sus." I visualized white light moving through my spine and central vessel with every inhale and through the top of my crown into my third eye with every exhale. After a time, the endless chatter of my mind ceased as I moved into a lighter space of consciousness: a space that allowed me to hear my crystals speaking. Their voices were faint; too small to make out their words. As I focused more, pieces of their conversation filled in.

"Let's _____ when he arrives."

"Who? What were they talking about?" My mind began chattering again; its recklessness jostled me from a higher awareness.

"Humans," a voice said with amusement. My concentration was lost and I had to start all over again.

"Je-sus... Je-sus... Je-sus." After a just a few moments this time, my body filled with light and there was a sensation of floating. My heightened awareness allowed a vision of the Angels surrounding my bed. Their white, heavenly bodies floated above me and filled the room with compassion and love. They were preparing; something was going to happen. My excitement almost ignited my mind into chatter again.

I commanded myself to, "Breathe now!"

"Je-sus... Je-sus... Je-sus."

Vivid colors and light began to circle into my eyes, I had the sensation of falling. With increasing speed and intensity, the lights penetrated my head and my eyeballs involuntarily rolled into their lids. My awareness was circling hard and fast into the space of my third eye. The pulsating, flashing and dancing colors of blue and purple continued to swirl until I fully arrived into my mind's eye. There they stopped and I had never been so comfortably aware.

I heard a voice ask me, "Can you hear me?"

"Barely," I answered.

A few more moments passed.

Again, the voice asked, "Can you hear me?"

This time I responded, "Yes. Who are you?" The crystals under my bed were buzzing with concentrated energy.

An image formed in front of me. I was overcome with a powerful and penetrating peace. I would not have believed what I saw, except that the power of love in me and in the room was encompassing, undeniable, strong, peaceful and gentle. There he was; Jesus, The King of Kings, The Almighty, The I Am.

"Jesus!" My inner voice cracked in amazement.

Without warning, a fear that I would lose my concentration pierced my heart; I would lose my chance to speak with my most beloved master.

"We will speak now and again," he said gently.

Every part of me was exposed to him. Jesus was looking directly into my soul. He embraced me; in his arms there was no judgment, only compassion.

Faced with the opportunity to gain incredible insight, my mind frantically formulated one billion questions. As soon as I was aware of them, they all melted away. Everything was happening exactly as it should; there were no concerns, fears or worries in this space. I was in peace.

"Father! My father it's really you," I cried joyfully.

"No. Brother"

"Brother? I have been taught all wrong."

Wasn't Jesus the Father?

The Prince of Peace let me ponder upon that for a minute before he said, "I have something to show you."

A clear image formed in my mind, it was Christ on the cross. Jesus was showing me his crucifixion. Every detail filed into my soul, it was a terrible, grotesque torture. As I watched in horror, my body twisted and writhed. Weeping then, I asked him to stop, I could not bear the brutality. There was so much pain.

Jesus did not pause; the scene continued. Mother Mary was crying for her son. I could feel every heart that was there that day, including Christ, his crucifiers and everyone who watched. I watched the anger filled eyes of the on-lookers as Christ suffered his torture. My spirit filled with grief and rage. The imprint of this horrible scene was so sharp; it was stinging my mind's eye. I struggled to shut it down.

Unable to stop it, I watched, felt and listened to Christ's persecution in all of its intensity. My body was now sweating, my head was pounding and I was exhausted from shaking and bawling. Angry and hurting I implored, "Why are you showing me this?"

Then it was over. The ugly vista lifted and I saw Christ in his glowing robe and crown again. My body smoothed, my mind rested and I said nothing for a moment. Still weeping, I just lied there.

Jesus quietly channeled peace back into me. His energy reclaimed my soul. Overwhelmed, by only a sliver of what Christ had actually experienced that day, I rested in his light. Jesus had just given me the gift of witness.

After a moment of recharging in the Holy Spirit, I found the strength to ask, "Jesus, I understand that you experienced terrible physical pain, but that must have been nothing compared to the emotional pain you felt. You loved them all so much and they returned your love with hatred."

"Yes," he proudly affirmed.

Jesus knew suffering; this was what he wanted me to understand. His purpose for showing me that awful scene was to make it clear to me that no one suffers alone. He is with every one of us, at every moment enduring all that we endure. His footsteps went before ours, so we would know that a path was carved for us.

In the past two years, I had prayed many times over my beloved Moe. My heart ached for him every day. We worked relentlessly to find healing, my faith never faltering because this knowledge was always in my heart. Jesus knew that our pain was acute; he knew of our suffering. Jesus had witnessed my every prayer. Maybe the Prince of Peace, The Healer of all healers would finally end our suffering.

As I rested and processed everything that had just happened, Jesus continued to channel for me. He sent the Holy Spirit through my energy systems, restoring me and endowing me with grace. The experience I shared with Christ that night had a profound effect on my consciousness. My relationship with him changed from one of blind faith to a real and tangible partnership; his existence in me was solidified.

In the next few days, I was awestruck and humbled. The feeling of being cherished and cared for in a way I had never known before remained. The inspiration that was left behind was something I wanted to share with everyone. The fear of rejection and disapproval kept my lips sealed. With only myself to reflect with, I realized that I really had been given a great gift. My most earnest hope was of seeing him again.

After that remarkable night, I embarked upon a new method of healing for Moe and myself. No longer would I use the massage table. The bed, surrounded by twelve crystals in a double Star of David pattern, became our sacred healing space. We were both comfortable and relaxed there and I was able to reach high states of consciousness inside the crystal grid. Moe was much more receptive to my work as he rested comfortably in a nest of blankets. There were no more power struggles; it was a nice change.

We practiced our new method of healing meditation often since I did not have to fight to keep him interested. Every night was an opportunity for miracles. On some nights, I was able to gain greater perspective on his condition as I removed pain and charged his systems. Other nights, I allowed myself the luxury of simply falling asleep peacefully.

On the nights when we weren't working or sleeping, we were talking. Those were some of our best times together. With no pressure to make a healing happen, I was able to really listen to and enjoy Moe. My boy had waited so long for me to hear him and I wanted to make it up to him. During those nights, I learned a lot about my friend. He had made plenty of observations in his seventeen years and was eager to tell me about them. He once told me, "Humans do a lot of stupid things to animals."

His insight was so clearly accurate, I had to laugh. "Humans do a lot of stupid things in general," I cleverly answered.

He did not find the topic or me funny at all. With a point-blank expression, he tore right into the subject. "You think you are so smart, you humans."

Picking up on his somber tone, I stifled my chuckles and asked him, "Have I ever done anything stupid to you?"

Moe wasted no time; he was ready to unload something. In my mind's eye, he showed me a picture of the time he had his teeth cleaned. It was only a year before. Our friend Lizz had convinced me that his teeth were in pretty bad shape. She warned that an infection could get into his heart and kill him. The risk of putting a sixteen-year-old cat under anesthesia was not something I was sure I could justify. Jeopardizing Moe's life in order to clean a few teeth seemed unnecessary. Lizz insisted the risk of heart attack was enough to warrant a cleaning.

Losing Moe to a heart attack was an incredibly scary thought. As I considered our choices, my fear of losing him grew. That fear motivated the wrong choice; I decided to get his teeth cleaned.

As I watched the scene replay, guilt, shame and disappointment in myself came crashing upon me. Moe was right: that was so completely stupid. I should have just let him be. Why fix what was not broken?

At the time, we had still been searching for the right vet. With no one to trust, I gambled that anyone could do a cleaning without screwing it up too badly. After all, it was a simple and routine procedure. We found a woman in the next town over who got him in right away.

After giving a brief health history and sharing my concerns with her, I explicitly directed this DVM not to use ketamines to anesthetize Moe. They were unnecessary and very harmful. Almost without any acknowledgement, she handed me a waiver. Her callous attitude should have tipped me off. Unfortunately, it didn't; I dropped Moe off and expected the procedure would go well.

Never intending to leave Moe alone, I drove to a park where I could meditate and send love to my friend. The bubbles of green heart energy I sent cocooned him. My meditation continued until the doctor called me to pick him up.

When I arrived, she handed me his release form. She had administered ketamines despite my request. Now completely infuriated, my face was red with the heat of anger. I forced myself to speak kindly. "You gave him ketamines?"

She responded with a tenuous and rehearsed answer about it being the only reasonable option.

I knew differently from my conversations with Lizz, my trusted professional friend. In fact, there were other, safer options.

"I asked you not to", I said. If you had no alternatives, you should have told me. I would have taken him somewhere else. This is my cat! You had no right to do that!"

The compulsion to scream at this stupid, inconsiderate woman was almost overpowering. A rich string of obscenities raced through my mind. My eyes spoke for me instead; they were shooting fiery daggers.

She responded with an indignant, smug expression and turned to retrieve my spaced-out friend. It was clear that she really did not care; my requests and concerns meant nothing to her.

This was exactly the kind of doctor we did not want. She had no regard for the highest good of her patients. I wondered how she had handled Moe throughout the procedure. Images of my buddy being tossed around like a rag doll flooded my head. After reluctantly paying the bill, I forcefully kicked the door open with my buddy in my arms. He was totally freaked out, loopy.

On the way home, it became even more obvious that Moe was hallucinating. He stared out the car windows with pupils as wide as the sun. He looked like a stoned, bobble head kitty, as he struggled to keep balance and focus on the world rushing by him. The car was tossing him like a clothes dryer. Moe was out of his mind; his head dipping back and forth and up and down as he tried to make sense of visual stimulation. We needed to get those drugs out of his system immediately. In response to my alarm, my foot pushed a little harder on the on the gas pedal.

When we arrived home, Moe wobbled and stumbled across the living room like a spaced-out hippie. After watching him for a minute, I carefully placed him in bed and began to search his chakras. His third eye was spinning. It was like an elliptical orbit wobbling off course. The chaotic energy siphoned off through my hands. It was spinning fast. Moe was on a merry-go-round. My anger increased as I felt what the drugs had done to him. He was hardly in his body, he was literally spaced-out.

After a few minutes, the energy of the ketamines left his body and the spinning ceased. Moe grounded back into his shell and gradually recognized his surroundings. He became aware of me and the work I was doing. He relaxed as I emptied the last of the narcotics and brought him back into balance. As he regained his full composure, the memory of me bubbling him in green surfaced.

"That was you?" he asked sweetly.

I kept working, "That was me, and I was with you the whole time."

"Thank you." He was relieved to return from his trip.

"You are okay now. Rest a bit buddy. You need it." With that, I left him to sleep.

Hours later, Moe woke up and had a bite to eat. He seemed all right and I had not thought of his teeth cleaning since that day. He was now reminding me of it. He was right, "Humans, indeed, do a lot stupid things to animals."

The vet's blatant disregard for Moe and lack of consideration for my requests to use a less invasive drug were an obvious violation and an act of extreme ignorance. It was as if she believed he really was a rag doll with no feelings, no emotions and no ability to perceive pain or panic. To her, Moe was nothing but a stuffed dollar sign.

My ignorance and stupidity were more obvious now that Moe had pointed them out. Like a fool, I chose to believe the terrifying thought of him dying because of the plaque on his teeth. Hoodwinked by fear, I placed my beloved in danger and caused him an undue trauma. It was a stupid thing to do.

Feeling like a big, fat, jerk, I reflected on the other times in my life when I allowed anxiety to induce careless, uninformed decisions. It came into my conscious that beliefs are like a diving board. They are the platform from which all actions spring. The diver is either moving with confident intention or fearfully flailing to some event. The resulting dive is delivered with grace or ends in a frenzied splash. Whatever I choose to believe has a direct effect on the events I create.

I observed myself repeating this effect many times, through many memories. Quite often, I dove gracefully. On other occasions, fear submerged me into an unwanted mess.

After listening to Moe, and reliving his trauma, I was inspired to no longer be hoodwinked by fear. Love would be the only platform and I would dive from it with grace. I would feel the air splitting from the tip of my nose as I descend into a perfect splash. By choosing love, I was going to stop doing "stupid things".

After ruminating on this lesson, I reminded Moe that I did help him recover from the drugs and that I had never intended for him to go through such an awful experience. "At least I pulled it all out of you. Doesn't that count for anything?"

"Yes, it does." I was getting used to his short, unfeeling answers.

The things my friend told me often made me feel as if I had failed him. Often, I had moved from fear. Moe was very critical of me; his pain was making him extremely irritable. He was downright cranky most nights. It was also his nature to be critical, however. From his vantage point, humans had a lot to learn and he had spent his years with an incredibly stubborn, and sometimes dense, member of the species.

Moe's crankiness and intolerance of my stupidity spawned another fear for me. With the belief that I had always taken incredibly good care of him collapsing, I asked my friend if he thought I had done good for him. Without hesitation, he complained that I once left him outside too long and his paws froze. Another memory surfaced in my mind. It happened when we were in college. I came home late from work and Moe was on the porch waiting. It was snowing and the temperature was below freezing. As soon as I pulled my car up and saw him, I knew he had been out too long. He darted through my feet into the house. Moe then found a warm corner and began licking his paws.

As I watched the memory unravel, I realized Moe was exposed to the cold long enough to get frostbite on the soft pads of his feet. It was a mild case, but enough to make him sensitive to any slight cold from then on. Moe had refused to step into any snow since then.

My heart sank. "I didn't know you were out. I don't know if I just forgot you or if somebody else let you out or what. I'm so sorry buddy."

Regret-filled tears soaked my face. Moe's response to my inquiry was unexpected. His poor paws. Had I done anything right for them? It seemed I had disappointed Moe quite often.

Fortunately, Moe accepted apologies easily. He had a remarkable ability to move on. All he needed was an opportunity to speak his grievances. An apology from me was always rewarded with renewed appreciation. The bitterness was dissolved and our hearts were cleared with every honest expression.

Around the time Moe and I were having our nightly conversations, Lizz told me about a kitty from the clinic that needed a home. Moe and I talked about adopting her. She was six months old and had never lived inside before.

"What do you think, Moe? Should we? Would you like a friend?" Moe was always very social with other animals; in the past, he enjoyed the company of many different friends.

"I don't know," he said. "I would have to meet her."

Hidden inside my heart, there was hope that a new kitty would stimulate Moe from depression and lethargy. The youthful energy of a kitten just might inspire my old friend to laugh and play again.

Moe seemed open to the idea of having a new friend, so I brought Lulu home and introduced them. She was a beautiful mix of orange, black and white; a petite little thing who carried too much fur for her body. Upon her arrival, Moe shared his food dish with her; he allowed it without thought or hesitation. This was the first time he had shared his food with anyone since Heather. It signified his acceptance of Lulu, the spark of hope in my heart ignited.

After Lulu finished eating, she went exploring her new home. Moe and I had a chance to talk without her hearing. Eagerly, I asked, "Well, what do you think?"

"She's really smart."

"She is?" I was pleased with his review. "Pretty cute, too, huh?"

Moe unenthusiastically walked off to his favorite spot on the rocking chair and drifted into sleep. He made no more comments as he excused himself from the conversation. Perhaps he was too tired and hurt too badly to really care at all.

In the weeks that followed Lulu and Moe began to bond. "She wants to have babies," he told me.

"Well, do it," I said.

"I can't." He was defeated.

"I know you can't make babies but you can still do it. You know, get it on." The conversation had me giggling again.

Moe was not giggling however. He removed himself from my immaturity. His irritation, frustration and anger were obvious. Moe's neutering was another operation he had not consented to; another stupid thing I had done.

Moe never allowed this to be discussed, the topic was forbidden. I asked myself how I could have made a better choice and avoided that violation yet still acted as a responsible pet owner. As I sympathized with Moe, I recognized that his neutering had caused another power leak. It was lurking in his energy system, resulting in weakness and disease. Since the topic of his neutering was off limits, I couldn't explore for any damage. His pride would not allow any intervention. According to Moe, that was another stupid human trick and he would not talk about it. Again, at a loss, I apologized once more.

Moe and Lulu got along well for a while. They cuddled and cleaned each other in Moe's favorite chair. Lulu had a lot of energy. Moe even played with her just a little bit. It seemed, at first, that adopting Lulu was good for Moe.

It was not long before things turned ugly, however. Lulu was a wild woman. She was tearing up my house. Every night, I woke up to the sounds of her destroying something. From my pillow, I would say to Moe, "Here she goes again. Why won't she just behave?"

Lulu was guilty of two offenses not taken lightly in my home; digging in my plants and knocking my crystals around. During those nights, I transformed into a raging lunatic. Like an ogre, I threatened and screamed repeatedly, "stop tearing up my house!"

After my voice was exhausted, my inner ogre surrendered. Screaming, shouting and losing my temper were all to no avail, so I tried talking with her. She explained that she had lived in a cage outside before and did not know how to live in a house.

My response was simple, "Lu if you have any questions, just ask Moe. He can teach you anything." It seemed like a wise way to deal with her.

It did not work. She continued to ransack my house maniacally for unsuspecting crystals. She knocked them down, tossed them and chased them. Some have never been recovered.

Things got worse when Moe confided in me that she had begun bullying him. That was the last straw. I was not going to let my sweetheart of a lifetime get hurt by a crazy, wild woman with bad manners. She had turned into a malicious pest. I talked with her again, this time explaining that if she hurt Moe she would not be allowed to live with us anymore.

The bullying stopped: however, Lulu continued to stalk the houseplants and toss the stones. I made sure she was outside all day as much as possible, hoping that by the time she came in, she would be too tired to make a pest of herself. Her manners improved very little. Our situation offered little escape; I loved her but I was also sorry I adopted her. Family is forever; giving her away would be inscrutable. We would just have to wait and hope she would mature nicely, until then she was our terrible, little monster friend.

Whenever Lulu was not terrorizing our nights, I worked and talked with Moe. My attempts at conversation and energy work were foiled by sleep more and more often. In fact, I was sleeping around eighteen hours a day. I chalked it up to depression; we were not getting very far in the way of miracles. My mental and physical health were beginning to suffer; I was exhausted from the struggle and pain of watching my beloved lose his health.

One evening, grace was delivered to us both. Whatever my original intention was for our evening, it fell to the wayside as I was guided to chant for Jesus. After only a few chants, my consciousness centered into my heart chakra. The pressure in the bedroom popped as he arrived.

"Jesus!"

He immediately began channeling into my third eye, saying nothing. I showed him my heart was heavy with worry over my kitty and I asked for help. He knew.

Jesus charged my energy systems, he was powerful and thorough. He delivered light through me with confident elegance. Unaware of his intention, I relaxed completely and openly received his love.

Then, Jesus instructed me to turn my attention to Moe. As I did, I discovered my vision was more clear than it had ever been; Jesus had expanded my consciousness and increased my frequencies.

Together, Christ and I channeled light through Moe.

When I moved through Moe's spine, Jesus warned, "Not too much." There was so much power moving through me, I was like an unmanned fire hose. Jesus showed me how to move gently, with intention, not force. I focused on the power moving through me, allowing it to flow smoothly and easily.

This beautiful lesson in color and light held me in a state of love and peace as I moved energy through Moe. Jesus was teaching me to stay in my heart chakra as I channeled energy. I was more expanded than I had ever been. My crown chakra was completely open; I was filled with light. It was a wonderful feeling. Moe was peacefully accepting our healing grace. We worked through my little kitty's physical body and chakra system until he was glowing, radiant with peace.

I thanked Jesus, perhaps too casually, before sleep took me.

I awoke the next morning expecting that Moe had made a full recovery. After all, Jesus is the ultimate healer. Moe was better. His improvement was obvious; his eyes were brighter and he was less stiff. However, he wasn't completely recovered. The ultimate healer had just blessed us with the most beautiful gift and I was confused. Why was there no grand, giant miracle? He should have been perfect, totally restored. I wrestled with my thoughts until I ached with exhaustion. The only choice left was to surrender and accept what had happened for what it was.

"We will see him again," I told myself, "I will work with Jesus again. We will get it."

Moe was better for a time. It was lovely to see him feeling better. Then the glow wore off and he was in pain and stiff again. I was working with him as much as I could. It seemed that I could not keep my eyes open anymore. Every time I attempted to channel with him, I would fall asleep after ten minutes and wake later to berate myself for failing again.

Meanwhile, Lulu was enjoying the freedom and excitement of being a young hunter. She was particularly adept at catching grasshoppers. She was an especially springy little acrobat. It was a pleasure to watch her.

One pleasantly sunny, spring afternoon, I was outside watching Lu when I heard a warning I did not heed. She was catching grasshoppers when something across the street caught her eye. I watched as she carelessly darted to the neighbor's yard. The same powerful voice rang loudly in my head, "Say good-bye."

I rejected it instantly. "No," I thought, "I did not just hear that. She will be back. I am just making it up because I am going crazy from stress."

Lulu's tail waved good-bye to me as she cruised through the tall grass.

She did not come home that night. The warning from the voice obsessed me.

The next day, I looked and called, but found nothing. A cloud of fear hung over me once again.

Why didn't I listen? She was gone and I had lost my chance to say good-bye. I fell into my bed, soaking my pillow with tears. Through my tears, I could see Moe staring at me from his nest in the closet. "Lu's gone," I wept.

Moe was tired. He did not take the news as I did. "Is this how you're going to act when I die?"

"No. I will be much worse. I will probably lose it. I will freak out, I am sure. Are you kidding? I cannot think about that. Don't say that!"

"You're being ridiculous," he answered without even a hint of emotion.

"Don't you care?"

"You don't see what I see," he replied.

"What do you see?"

He closed his eyes and he returned to his nap. I wondered how he could be so callous. What did he see? I cried into my pillow until sleep found me again.

Hours later I awoke, still upset. Anger was eating at me. Why didn't I listen to that guiding voice?

I closed my eyes again to concentrate on meditation. There were questions that desperately needed answers. Despite her inability to live peacefully inside our home, I still loved her and I needed to know what happened.

The light began to fill me as my meditation took root. Peace and order slowly returned to my mind. As I fell deeper into a peaceful state, I continued to ask my Angels to show me what happened. Minutes later, a tragic scene unfolded in my mind's eye.

Lu crept into the neighbor's yard, on the hunt for their chickens. She failed to notice a pack of dogs as she crossed under the fence. They closed in on her. She tried to outrun them, there were five on her tail. One grabbed her. A fight over her little body ensued. She was gone. It happened fast.

Horrified then, a heated rage flushed my every cell. What an awful end. Lu must have been terrified. I wanted to shoot those dogs. They were a neighborhood menace, barking at everything that passed by. Neglected in their fenced yard, they became a wild pack. They tore at Lu's flesh like feral beasts. Unable to watch any longer, I arose from the meditation enraged and distraught. This was not an answer I wanted or expected. This answer delivered no peace or closure.

Moe accepted Lu's fate casually, as if the news of her passing was of no significance at all. I was mad at him. "Don't you care?" I asked.

Again, he answered, "You don't see what I see."

"What do you see?"

He answered with a sigh of frustration. He could not explain what he saw. It was too much and maybe I would not have understood.

Lu's death could not be allowed to halt my attempts at healing Moe. It was right back to business for us. Moe was hurting more and moving less. Our situation was becoming more dire than I would have ever predicted.

As I fell asleep one night, I asked for a dream that would give me some insight into Moe that would heal him.

An Angel answered me. She was beautiful. Her long blonde hair flowed from under a golden crown. In her hands, she carried some sort of tool I could not see. Peace and love emanated from her. She wore a pink gown and spoke clearly, "King. He wants to be called King." That was all. The image of her faded away.

The next morning, I remembered the dream perfectly. Its quality was different from my other dreams; it was thick with reality. I walked into the living room to find Moe resting in his favorite chair. "Good morning, King."

He lifted his head in surprise and asked, "How did you know I wanted to be called that?"

"I had a dream. A lady told me."

His eyes were wide as he stared back at me. A moment of peace passed between us. He was delighted. So was I.

Moe's desire to be called King was never explained. Maybe he thought his original name was undignified, though he never complained. Maybe the name King appealed to his pride. It was more than that though; perhaps he really was royalty. His path had not been easy, it included so much suffering. Through all of his pain, a great task was achieved. So much had changed between us since he was a kitten; much of my own evolution into enlightenment could be credited to King. Clearly it was a title he deserved. From that point on, everyone was informed of his new name and how to address him properly.

Weeks later, while cleaning, I found King hiding in the closet. He looked up and asked me," Why can't I feel my legs?"

The answer was obvious to me, I just could not tell him the truth.

"I don't want to live like this," he cried.

After petting him a bit, I left to think where he could not hear me.

Quietly, I sat on the patio. Our nightmare had just intensified. King was losing feeling in his hind legs. Soon, he would not be able to walk. I struggled with my thoughts, trying to prevent my erratic emotions from blocking logic. The nerves feeding his legs had finally, completely atrophied. Dr. S. would not be able to do anything. Healing him was my responsibility alone and I was running out of time. We needed Jesus; he was the only one who could help us.

That night, I took King with me to bed. The music was set and the stones were charged for meditation. I called upon Jesus again. Sleep was aggressively creeping in on me. A battle to keep my awareness from drifting into slumber ensued. King needed me, sheer will kept my exhaustion at bay.

Jesus entered without any announcement. Immediately relieved and revived by his arrival, I motioned to King. Christ looked upon us for a moment, and then spoke. "Rest now," he said. "Call on me again in two weeks."

Every part of me desperately needed rest: Jesus was right about that. Waiting for two weeks to take action was not rational however. Our situation needed immediate attention; so why was I told to wait?

A break from all of the stress would bring me relief. But what about King? His mobility would soon be compromised.

With much apprehension, I followed Jesus' advice. For the next two weeks, I made no attempts at healing my buddy. As those weeks went by King became weak. His legs refused to do as he asked them. He spent most of his time sleeping in the closet. He could no longer jump up to the bed or his rocking chair. All of his favorite places were now past his reach. It was happening so quickly. Witnessing his deteriorating condition was unbearable. My beautiful friend was miserable and now relied on me for everything.

The end of our two-week wait finally came. On the morning of the fourteenth day since I had last spoken with my brother in light, I did not hesitate to call on him again. I left King resting in the closet and prepared the massage room.

With crystals and gems surrounding me, and the massage table under me, I chanted and breathed "Je-Sus". Instantly, he was there by my side. He had been waiting for me.

"Jesus we have to heal King! His legs aren't working!"

The next words came gentle and firm: "King is dying."

The words flooded me with terror. I resisted.

"No. No. No. No. No. No. No. No. No. No! We have to heal him."

He asked for my hand. I held out my left hand and felt him take it up into his. He was now channeling into me. His love, comfort and infinite compassion funneled into me. After a minute, he spoke, "Kerry, sometimes when you want someone to heal, you have to let them go."

I fought his words. There was a mountain of resistance in me. "No!" I cried.

Jesus held strong and calm. He channeled into me a bit more, his love was grounding me. I relinquished in tears. "How long?" I asked.

"Not long. One season."

I remembered Moe would be turning eighteen soon, was that what he meant by season?

"What do I do?" I asked.

"Enjoy him. Love him and spend your time."

Bawling, afraid and devastated, I jumped from my table and ran to the closet to find my friend. My head landed on the blankets beside him. He said nothing to me. He knew I knew. My tears rained on us both. Would they would ever stop? How could I ever let him go?

In the weeks that followed, I did just what Jesus had told me. King and I spent as much time together as we could. We talked every night and spent our days napping and snuggling. In between my tears came very little acceptance of what was to come. I asked King if there was anything he wanted from me, anything he wanted me to do.

His answer was unexpected, "Quit smoking. It is preventing you from riding your bike. It's stopping all your fun."

His insights into my own health and happiness surprised me. He was right. My bad habits were causing me to lose precious playtime and were compromising my health. He had watched me lose my balance in the last few years. I thought about all of the grief and stress his death was going to cause me. I would not dare attempt quitting for a while.

Selfishly, I told him it was a lot to ask. He scoffed at me. There were things he did not understand about being human. He expected my will to be as strong as his. I doubted that it was.

My refusal to honor King's request left me feeling even more unworthy and useless. He was on his deathbed and he was still thinking of me; his last request was that I act to love myself. In my stupid human-ness, I could not deliver.

I asked him again, "Is there anything I can do for you? Can I get you anything? Would you like something special to eat?"

"Tuuuunaaa." His request was surprisingly emphatic.

He loved tuna. So often, through the years, he had come running when a can was opened.

Delighted by his request and the memories of his darting into the kitchen seeking his favorite snack, I answered, "Sure sweetie."

That turned out to be his last meal. He ate it enthusiastically, purring loudly until the whole can was finished. I watched him happily, petting him as he ate for the last time.

"Thank you," he purred.

Two days later, I attempted to coax King into a meal with some fresh roast beef from the deli. He smelled it and then turned his head. "No, but thank you, it smells delicious."

We were close. His body would shut down soon with no food or water. I was in an altered state that lingered between denial and fear and acceptance of what was to come. My friend was dying. There was nothing I could do to stop it. I was grateful he would feel so much better soon, but it was too soon for me. Living life without him seemed impossible and unbearable. He had been my constant companion for eighteen years. I watched him grow up and then grow old. He was there for me at every turn in my life. Our bond was only strengthened by the events of the last few years. I was closer to him than anyone, any person in my life. Losing him was filling me with more grief than I had ever imagined possible. The thought of losing my best friend had me more concerned with my own future than his impending journey to the other side.

The next morning I woke to King's terrible screams. He had never made those painful screeches before. I flew from my bed to find him. He was on his back, in a corner, in the living room, behind the couch. His breathing was labored, his eyes wide with terror. Gently and calmly, I placed my hands on him. We breathed together until the pain passed. When it was over, I made him comfortable on his kitty bed and placed him in front of the couch.

"King, I need to go to the store. I'll be back as soon as I can."

"You're leaving me?" He was afraid death would come while I was gone.

"There is something important I have to get."

King had just suffered a heart attack and I did not recognize it. My overwhelming grief was blinding me to his condition. Thinking of myself and my need to preserve my memory of King, I made the decision to leave my friend because I needed film for the camera. In eighteen years together, we had taken very few pictures together. It was an insensitive decision. I was blind to his fear.

"I'll be back soon, don't worry."

Somehow, I navigated the store quickly, though I could barely see through my tears. My feet were carrying me and my hands were working to complete my task, but my mind was not there. The haze of grief and fear of the inevitable shadowed my very soul into complete darkness. The autopilot inside of me found what I needed and drove me home; a drive I do not remember.

King was relieved when I returned. His relief was short lived however; the aggravation of picture taking was a very inconsiderate nuisance. None of those pictures looked very good. He looked so ill and I was a mess. Regretfully, I realized my total disregard and gave up after he asked me to stop. The flash was bothering him and he was rightfully disturbed by my disrespect. He needed to rest and be comforted.

"Okay King, I'm sorry. I have so few pictures of you. I want to remember you. I want to remember everything, all of your colors, patterns and stripes."

King was weak, he had no response. He rested his body into his pillow and closed his eyes. Up above him, on the couch, I too fell asleep. I wanted desperately to stay awake and treasure the little time I knew was left, but my exhaustion betrayed me. We were close to death; I did not realize how close. As I drifted off, I questioned if we would make it through the weekend. What would I do with his body if we did not? Would we make it to Monday when I could take it to the crematorium?

A few hours later, I awoke to the realization that King had heard my recent thoughts about disposing of his body. He was aware of all my worries. How dreadfully awful to hear your loved one struggling to decide what to do with your body when you are gone. Those were thoughts I did not want him to hear, he shouldn't have been troubled. King was doing all he could to hold on as long as he could for my sake. He was sacrificing his comfort and himself for me. Even though he was dying, again, my well-being was still his greatest concern. This was enough to shake me out of my self-pity. I would not ask him to hold on any longer. His suffering had been too long and too terrible.

I spoke gently to him, "King, if you need to go, then go. I will figure out what to do with your body. Please, don't worry about that."

He opened his eyes in response to my words, they swelled with love and gratitude.

King was so weak then, he could not even lift his head. My final act as his care taker and friend would be to simply keep him comfortable. I charged and programmed some crystals to keep him in peace and free of pain. After gridding them around his pillow, I petted and rubbed my beautiful King in all of his favorite spots. All that really mattered then, was that he was going home.

As I petted his soft fur, I cried, "What will I do with out you? I wish I was going with you."

"No. You are going to go on to be an amazing healer. You are going to have a family. I'm going to watch you."

His insights ignited my will to go on for just a moment. "How do you know that?"

"You don't see what I see." He said.

I thought about that until I heard him speak again. "Will you pray for me?"

I suddenly realized I had not considered how frightened he might be. Why hadn't I prayed for his safe, peaceful and painless transition? Death is a journey into the unknown. He must have been terrified.

The words I spoke next were poured through me by channel. A prayer flowed from my lips so elegant it could have only come from divine inspiration. I called the Angels to carry King from this life into the next. He would feel no pain, only joy and relief as he entered Heaven, the trumpets playing for his return. All of Heaven would rejoice and his beloved friends and family would be there to greet him. My prayer was not a request, it was a declaration. I spoke those words with absolute authority, knowing that they were true. As that prayer was delivered, it was simultaneously answered. My home became filled with the peaceful and tangible presence of a powerful love. King would have a peaceful, easy and even a joyous passing.

After I finished, I felt my friend relax. He said only, "wow." His fears were completely abated. I had never uttered a prayer so powerful before in my life and have never said one since.

After praying for King's easy passage home, I asked God to turn my house into a sanctuary of peace. My request that we be surrounded with the Holy Spirit and the Angels we needed was answered immediately. My home began buzzing, the air was instantly charged with their presence.

Fully engaged in ceremony then, I realized I had one candle with very little wax left. Suddenly, it became important to me that the candle would light and stay lit. It represented the presence of the Holy Spirit; we needed it to complete this journey. Silently, I asked Jesus to keep the candle burning.

Christ whispered into my left ear, "I will keep it lit until..."

"Until what?" I asked.

Shocked by his answer, and by his presence, I was unable to hear all of what he said.

"Until what?"

There was no answer.

It was coming. It would be easy. It was going to be miraculous and graceful. We are all so loved that a journey like this could only be a blessed and beautiful homecoming.

"King, do you believe in miracles?" My question was inspired by my reflection upon our last few years together. We had worked so hard for a miracle. We never lost our faith and in the face of death, we were still asking for more miracles.

His answer was the sweetest thing I have ever heard anyone say, my heart spilled as King spoke.

"It was a miracle the day you came to get me." A geyser of emotion exploded from my chest, more tears carved through the already worn path down my face.

I remembered that day eighteen years ago. When I rescued King from that shelter and brought him home, into my life and into my heart, everything changed. Because of that day, because spirit brought us together, because an idea came to my mother to go and get him, King had a chance to love and be loved, something he may never have gotten. That day King found his place by my side and I found a friend who had blessed me and taught me more than I could have ever imagined. That was a miracle. We had shared eighteen years of a beautiful journey since then. The love, laughter, tears and lessons we shared together were invaluable. King had changed me, improved my awareness and opened my heart and mind to new possibilities. He would be in my heart forever.

Now we were here, at the end of our journey together and I was sending him home. One season, just like Jesus said. Our lives together had come full circle.

Then, I spoke the words I had spoken to him so many times in all of our years together, "I love you so much Moe-Moe. I just love you. I'm so glad for our time together. I'm going to miss you so much. What will I do without you?"

"I will be with you. I will be..." His voice trailed off. He was asking someone where he would be watching me from. Though I listened ferociously for the answer, I could not hear.

King spoke again after a minute, "Thank you for taking such good care of me, especially the last few years."

My tears began spilling again. "Of course, my buddy, I'd do it over again if I had to."

We both knew what we had just been through was something neither of us ever wanted to ever go through again. It was so incredibly hard on us both. None of that mattered now. He was on his way home. Soon his suffering would end.

Hours later, I awoke when the candle light went out. I reached down and felt King's body. He was no longer there. I panicked and felt it again.

"No!" I screamed.

It was lifeless; there was no breath. My eyes moved to the space above his body where they found a blue bubble floating, moving upwards.

Next, I heard the words, "Kerry, I made it!" It was King, my beloved friend. It was the same voice. Only now, it was different; lighter, unburdened.

I jumped up in shock and disbelief; my hands cradled my own head. He was gone? Did this just really happen? It was done, over. Shock, anger and grief took me all at once, pulling me into darkness. It was impossible to pay attention to the voice, the bubble or anything besides the torrent of pain that had just shattered my heart.

Without any thought to drive my actions, I numbly wrapped King's body in his blanket and moved it under the air conditioner. It was almost five a.m., June twenty eight, two thousand eight and my best friend had just passed.

My Angel was loudly insisting that I go into meditation. I ignored him. How the hell would I be able to get into any kind of meditative space at this point? I went outside to my porch instead and smoked about a thousand cigarettes.

Outside I sat, moving between overwhelming states of grief and a dulling, numbing denial. All the while, the birds were singing to greet the new day that was dawning. How dare they sound so alive? So inspired? Didn't they know that the end of joy forever had just come?

My Angel told me again, "Go into meditation."

Completely depleted then, I agreed, thinking I would just fall asleep anyway. As I walked back inside, I saw King's body and wondered if it would keep for a day. Seeing his empty body lay there was surreal, a detail of death that demanded I move out of denial.

I fell into my bed, my head hurting, my emotions spinning, my thoughts circling between the past and future. I began to breathe deeply in an attempt to channel light and peace into myself. Much to my amazement, a state of peace soon found me. A quell in tears allowed me to hear a small voice calling me. I strained to hear it.

"Kerry, Kerry I made it!"

"King, is that you?" In my mind's eye, I saw him approach. He was a kitten again. He was so bright, full of energy and joy.

"I brought you a present!" His enthusiasm was almost silly.

"What is it?" I asked, then partly in shock and partly in laughter.

"A mouse. We do not kill them here. We only catch them!"

I smiled at his childlike delight. "How do you feel, honey?"

"I feel great! My back is great! I have no pain!"

Then he looked at me intently. He studied my body for a minute and then spoke to someone I could not see or hear. "She has pain too."

I asked my friend if he saw Lulu. "Mmmhmmm. She's right here!"

Immediately, Lu came into view. Her little body was as fluffy as I had remembered. "Lu, what happened?" Her little voice told me how she had gone to chase a chicken and did not see the dogs coming.

She kept telling me, "I couldn't get away". She told me the traumatic story without any sense of distress. She was okay.

Again, I sensed a voice talking with King. "Oh," he answered.

To my mind's eye, King delivered a picture of his body. "Don't worry about that. It is like an old t-shirt. It can't be worn anymore."

With King's direction, some of my attachment to his body left. "Okay." I said.

Again, I heard someone speaking to my friend. King took another hard look at me and then told me he had to go because I needed to rest.

"Will I see you again?" I asked sorrowfully.

He only smiled in response.

Unbelievably, I fell asleep. King was right, rest was in order. I was more exhausted than I had ever been. Later when I awoke again, the reality that my friend was gone smacked me in the face and my tears began running again. The events that had transpired in the last six hours had left me shaking. My thoughts ran back and forth through all that had happened. The unexpected visit from King was incredibly comforting; however, I was still hurting. King was in Heaven, he was healed. He was having a great time and felt better than he had felt in a long time. He was with his family and friends. He was in the presence of the All One. All of this was true and all of this comforted me. Still, my heart was broken and bleeding. King was in spirit, but I was left behind on this physical plane, mourning for the loss of him. I longed to hold him and pet him again. There was no end to the pain, my chest caved in with a huge gaping hole.

The morning light came filtering through the window and I awoke to the task of taking care of King's body. My soul most wanted to give it back to the earth, but I could not bear to think of ever leaving his body behind. The memory of King's directions from the morning before echoed in my mind, "an old t-shirt". King was right, it really did not matter what I chose to do. The body was broken and no longer had any use. Despite that logic, I was nonetheless emotionally attached to his body and needed to keep it close. Someday, I wanted to give him a memorial that I would never have to leave.

An enormous amount of calm resolve built up inside me. It lent me the strength to move King's body to my car. The autopilot inside me had come out again. It was taking care of things so I didn't have to. To our favorite vet clinic she drove and I did not shed one tear.

Dr. S greeted me, "Hey Kerry. What's going on?"

"I need to do something with King's body." My voice was weak but I was calm.

His eyes changed. "King died?"

"Yes, Saturday night. He was ready to go. He had several heart attacks and then went gracefully." Still no tears.

Lizz came out from the back. She immediately hugged me. "Do you want me to go get him?"

"No, no. I can do it." It was as if I was being carried; someone else was doing all of this. I was not in my body; I was comfortably numb.

"This is not me," I thought, as I walked out to the car. "I cannot believe I am doing this right now."

As I carried the body past Dr. S, he was crying just a little. He had stepped outside for a moment to catch his breath. I was touched by his genuine emotion and again felt grateful that he had been our veterinarian. He really did care. Strangely, I wanted to tell him everything was in divine order and there was no need for tears. I moved past him instead, pretending not to notice.

Lizz met me in the back room. She had already called the crematorium. She lifted the blanket for one last look. "He looks good! He looks peaceful."

"We were blessed with a beautiful passing. He transitioned with grace." I explained.

Lizz smiled sweetly and left me to say my last good-byes.

I looked down on that old t-shirt, memorizing the colors and stripes. My eyes traced his face and nose. My hands reached down to hold his paw and I realized that I could not let go. A flood of tears came rushing, my heart was bleeding again. The skin on the pads of his feet was so soft; I would never feel them again.

Then I heard a voice from somewhere above me. It spoke loudly, "Look at what she is doing!"

Another voice responded, "Huh? Oh."

It was my friend. It was King! He was with me again! Someone was instructing him to take notice of me.

"Kerry, you have to let go." King directed me gently.

"I can't," I cried. "I can't!"

"You have to."

I stood there, still rubbing his paw. While I traced the soft, round pads, my friend was talking to me from somewhere above me. King was not in that old body; King was not what I was holding onto. I felt King's presence and heard him speaking and still I wanted to hold on to that old t-shirt.

The tears continued to spill and my thoughts pulsed, "this isn't King, this is just his body".

King was right, I had to let go. By sheer will and in less than a second I achieved an act of bravery. I dropped his paw and covered the body, leaving the room without looking back.

King followed me. His pride and relief for me was evident, it danced on my shoulders.

In complete hysterics, I drove myself home. "Now this is me," I thought, "this is more of what I expected."

The next days went on much in the same way. Whenever I was crying, King would come to comfort me. Being bereaved by King's passing and also relieved by the powerful truth he was finally healed left me in a strange, confused state. My great sadness was punctuated by King's comforting visits and I was grateful to know he was happy and healthy again. Even so, I could not align my heart and mind to understand all of what had transpired. King had gone home; I could not see him on earth anymore. He had not died however. He was more alive than ever, just different. I struggled in agony between his visits.

As that first week went by, I noticed King's presence in other animals. His likeness was in dogs, squirrels, cats and every animal that came across my path. At first, I was mystified; how he could be in them and still be in spirit? Eventually, I realized that I was experiencing his consciousness in everything. King was one with everything, his consciousness had completely expanded.

After the shock of his death wore off, I stopped noticing King's presence in all other animals. He visited less and less. I carried on with my days, struggling with my overwhelming grief. Life kept moving. I had to keeping moving too.

The past two years of acting as caretaker to my best friend had put a mass of stress on me. The constant worry over King caused a physical response in my body. A visit with my homeopathic doctor turned up a diagnosis of mononucleosis. Not only was I emotionally exhausted, I was physically exhausted as well.

During the last six months of King's life, I was sleeping around eighteen hours a day. I had routinely beaten myself up for repeatedly falling asleep when I attempted to meditate and channel for King. It never occurred to me that through all the stress, fear, worry and pain, I had actually manifested a physical illness. That physical illness matched and mirrored my emotional and mental symptoms. I was absolutely spent on every level, there was nothing left to me.

It was time to take care of myself; two years of ignoring my own body and needs had caught up with me. Everything I had went to healing and taking care of King. My cup needed filling.

Surviving King's passing was so difficult, I was not sure I would ever heal. At the very least, I was anticipating a long recovery. Spirit had other ideas for me.

Just months after King had gone home, while I was vacuuming, I heard a voice ask, "Kerry, what color?"

"Oh no, no way! I'm not ready! My heart is still aching!" I scolded the voice. My Guides and Angels were attempting to send me a new friend.

The thought of that scared me to the point of shaking. I couldn't allow it.

"Don't you dare!"

"Kerry, what color?" They insisted.

"UGGGGGHHHHH… black and white." My answer surprised me, it just fell out.

I had all but forgotten about this until a few days later. There I was, sitting in my chair, watching TV, when I looked out the window for no particular reason. At first, I could not believe my eyes. I looked harder.

"Oh my God!"

I jumped from my seat and ran into the front yard. There sat a tiny black and white kitty staring across the road, wondering where he should go. I scooped him up into my arms and brought him inside.

"You are unbelievable!" I reprimanded my Angels.

It was no use, by then I was already snuggling this new little kitty.

"What's your name?" I asked.

"I don't have a name," he answered.

"Then you also don't have a home. You can stay with me." Another decision had just happened so fast, in an instant, without a thought or a consideration. It was done. I had a new friend.

God gave me another gift and I swore I was not ready. I swore I would never love someone so much again. Thankfully, God knew better.

Beyond King

*B*eing so blessed to share eighteen years with such a good friend, I have often pondered our lives together. Paying two dollars for someone who was so infinitely invaluable, who influenced my life so deeply, in so many ways, was miraculous. I am eternally grateful to King, for his gifts of loyal friendship, unconditional love, abundant patience and amazing wisdom.

King gave me an enormous amount of perspective in his last few years. I am thankful for every conversation we shared. Every insight I gained by listening to him is precious. He introduced me to a world that would have been beyond my reach without him.

Animals are true masters of unconditional love. My experiences with King taught me that repeatedly. He was very forgiving of me. He chose to love me, no matter what. Mastering unconditional love is no small undertaking. Having never met a human who has mastered unconditional love, I wonder how it comes to animals so easily.

Inspired by all that I learned from working and speaking with King, I began speaking with other animals. I practiced conversation and healing with cats, dogs, squirrels, deer, pigs, birds and occasionally other animals.

Being a master of unconditional love sometimes requires the occasional pardoning of bad behaviors or neglect. One hopes that these instances are incidental or accidental. Unfortunately, that is not always true.

I spoke briefly with a cat once about his unfair and abusive living conditions. I was visiting with some friends, sitting on their patio, when he rubbed up against me. This cat, Crash, was particularly vocal. As I petted his soft, long fur, he began to tell me a story I was not expecting.

He told me his owner had thrown him down the stairs and told him to stay in the basement. He was not allowed to come upstairs anymore. Astonished by what he said, I asked him to continue his story.

Crash enjoyed my attentive listening and petting as he further unloaded his anger and frustration. His tails of abuse and neglect continued for a while. He had endured quite a lot of verbal and physical assaults. I had no immediate ideas on how to handle the situation; there was no advice to give. Clearly, the cat did not wish to live out his life in the cold, dark basement. Clearly, he desired the affection of a more loving keeper.

I held him in my arms wondering how I could help. Before I could stop them, the words escaped my lips, "Do you want to come live with me?"

He howled an emphatic "Yes!" He came home with me that night. Crash was delighted when I called him to bed later that evening. "I get to sleep in the bed?" he asked.

I answered, "Things will be different here, young man."

Crash ran away weeks later. He had fallen in love with a neighbor barn cat and decided to make a home with her. Crash found his own solution to his problems: he had also found love.

Crash demonstrated to me that our animal friends' ability to love unconditionally is not without boundaries. He was not a doormat. He loved himself enough to find an escape from his abusive situation. He reminded me that practicing unconditional love does not mean repeatedly enduring abuse. Though he forgave his keeper, he would not forget what happened. He chose to move on. He chose wisely in my opinion. Things were not likely to change.

I knew another friend who could not forget. Almost accidentally, I stumbled into conversation with her. Her keeper was a friend named John. What she told me made me sick to my stomach. I was visiting John, in his home, when I noticed how his dog was leering at him. She was paranoid and afraid. I had always known John to be very generous and fun loving. I loved him dearly and his dog's behavior was unsettling.

When John left the room, I called his dog Bella over to me and asked what was wrong. In my mind's eye, she showed me a picture of another dog. I listened and watched. She told me his name. He was a large rottweiler, they had grown up together. I had never met this dog. Patiently, I waited for her story to unfold.

What she told me next tore through my solar plexus like lightening. She sobbed to me, "He shot him!"

I reasoned with her, "What? No. I do not believe it. There must have been something wrong. A good reason for his action. There must be something you don't understand."

How could John murder his own dog? It must have been a mercy killing: the dog must have been terribly sick or injured.

She asked me, "How can I trust him?"

I had no answer.

"I'm so sorry, Bella. It is easy to see why you don't trust him." I attempted to convince her that she was loved dearly and had no reason to fear John. She refused any comfort. Bella lived in fear for her life. Bella needed to be healed; she needed the trauma removed from her home life. I could not confront my friend however; he had never spoken about it.

The situation had me stifled until I found the opportunity to ask my friend's brother what had happened. He told me the rottweiler had bitten a roommate's dog. After that, the roommate delivered an ultimatum: the rotty could not stay. My friend was financially busted. John had nowhere to go and no money to get him there. He thought the only choice was to end the rottys life.

As the story unraveled, I was overcome with emotion. My heart went out to all of them. I wished my generous and jovial friend had found a better solution. What he did haunted him and destroyed his relationship with his remaining dog.

I found myself at a loss for what to do. There was no fixing this. Bella had witnessed the murder of her beloved pal by the hands of her once-trusted keeper. In a later conversation with her, I explained why John had made that choice. It was useless; she would accept no reason. It was unfair to ask her for forgiveness. Unconditional love has its limits. For Bella, it stopped at murder. She refused to forgive or forget. I loved Bella up and prayed God would bring her relief. It was all I could do.

Often, I see that people assume that their friends are unaware of what is said and done. On the contrary, our friends are aware of everything we think, say or do. When I first heard Bella describe her situation, I was sure she had misunderstood something; she had missed some subtle detail. Unfortunately, she was aware of everything that happened. Her perceptions were quite accurate.

My cat Blackie is another example of an animal who exhibits a keen and perceptive mind. Months after King had died, I moved to a new house. I believe moving me from my prior home was Spirit's way of helping me move on in my life. Away from the place that held my last memories of King, I was better able to make new memories.

Blackie came out from under my porch one morning. He was a lovely surprise. We fell in love immediately. He was the brother of my current cat, Fineas. Apparently, the owners of the barn next door were not concerned about the current problems with cat overpopulation. Apparently, they had never watched The Price is Right. Despite Bob Barker's efforts, they allowed their cats to breed freely.

Blackie had a very strong presence of dignity as King had. He was a wise one. Blackie heard my every thought. After listening to me, on one occasion, he scolded me for beating myself up.

He had been lying next to me as I was meditating. He listened while I berated myself for a mistake I once made. I was being overly demanding and judgmental towards myself, a chronic habit of mine.

He spoke to me bluntly, as I stirred in my bed, "You are being too hard on yourself."

I thought for a moment. He stared at me.

"You're right, Blackie. Thanks for telling me."

His insight helped me step out of the circle I was spinning. I remember Blackie's words whenever I slip back into that habit.

Blackie's keen awareness and ability to convey his perceptions about me are evidence of his intellect and wisdom. I had underestimated Blackie before that day. He proved himself wiser than I had judged.

Blackie was with me less than a year before he was hit by a car. My still grieving heart was broken all over again. Why would God send me a friend, so soon after I lost King, and then take him away, so suddenly and unexpectedly? Eventually, I accepted it. It was just an accident. God did not do it. Blackie was there to share his love with me, when I needed it. He had fulfilled the purpose of his life.

Lizz's dog Iris was a beautiful example of loyal friendship, unconditional love and a keen intelligence. She loved Lizz selflessly. After many years together, it came time for Iris to go home. Lizz called me to come to her aid. After all that she had done for King, I was glad to help her in any way that I could. On the way to her house, I recounted how she had saved King's life.

Iris was hurting terribly. She had cancer. The first thing she said to me, when I tuned into her energy was, "when will I die?" She was ready to go. Iris was extremely tired. She did not want me poking around in her energy field.

"It won't be long before the Angels come to get you Iris. I will not interfere with your process."

Iris asked, "Why does my foot hurt?"

I scanned her body and energy field finding that her blood vessels were swollen and irritated from a steroid injection.

"Iris, Lizz has given you some medicine to help, you are sore from the injection. May I help there?"

With her confusion relieved and my trust gained, I proceeded to siphon her pain. Then I asked Iris if there was anything she wanted to tell Lizz.

"Have you ever seen eyes so blue?" she asked me sweetly. I did not understand.

She asked me again. "Have you ever seen eyes so blue?"

Iris and I continued talking as I worked to make her comfortable. The prednisone was really making her irritable; she barely tolerated my work. After I siphoned off the pain, I attempted to go into her chakras for some deeper work.

She pushed me out and then asked, "Can we be done now?" It was her way of telling me that, in fact, we were done.

I spoke words of comfort and reassurance to Iris, "It will all be over soon. Your journey home will be easy. You are a good girl, Iris. Lizz loves you very much."

Lizz was doing her best to keep from breaking down. When I told her what Iris said about her blue eyes, she dropped the dish she was washing and looked at me in shock, astonished by my words.

Iris had one blue and one brown eye. Lizz told me how she had often told Iris how beautiful her eyes were. In their many years together, Lizz had repeated this lovely term of endearment to Iris time and time again. Iris was listening and she wanted to tell Lizz that her eyes were beautiful too. She had stared into them since she was a pup, also pondering their hue. Those words touched my friend deeply; they conveyed profound love and loyalty.

A few days later Lizz left a thank you card in my door. Inside it, she enclosed a dried iris flower. Her note expressed her gratitude to me and for the words I was able to speak for Iris. She had known exactly what to say.

Often, I have witnessed my animal friends staring at things most humans do not see. The first time I noticed this was when King informed me there was a ghost with us on the patio of our former Colorado home. Since then, I have noticed other animals watching things my eyes cannot yet see. My current cat, Fineas, was just a baby snuggling on my chest one night when his eyes grew wide. He slowly backed himself off of me and out of the room.

Just months after King's passing, Fineas and I were living in a home I had recently moved in to. This house was very busy energetically. Blue flashes of light were whizzing by me all throughout the house but I had not found any time to investigate them. Fin's reaction to whatever it was that he saw caused me to procrastinate no longer. I closed my eyes and began to meditate. Immediately, my chest felt heavy. There was a weight on it causing me to have difficulty breathing.

Someone was repeating, "Can you see me? Can you see me?"

Startled as I was, I kept my ground and continued to look. I became aware of more of them; my room was filled with many tiny presences. There was a larger one behind me. He asked me to move my bed. He said I would sleep better. Still, I could not see who was talking and wasn't sure if they could be trusted. They felt happy and excited, eager for me to notice them. Their energies were vibrating so fast. Their words were kind; they radiated gently. They had been trying to get my attention for days. Whizzing and twirling all around me was their attempt to catch my eye.

After listening and feeling for awhile, my anxieties calmed and I was able to ask what they were. They spoke of trees and plants. I listened patiently. They were all talking at once. I asked, "Please one at a time. It is very difficult to hear."

One male voice spoke then; he told me he was king.

"King of what?"

"I am the king of the faeries that live here. We take care of the trees."

Now convinced that I was completely off my rocker, I was tempted to throw this experience away. But I could not disbelieve; what was happening was very real. I struggled to maintain the sense and order I had assigned to my world. Faeries were not real. That is why we call them fairytales. I struggled to discard this new reality, but to no avail. For crying out loud there was one still sitting on my chest!

Laughing aloud I proclaimed, "Okay my house is full of faeries, this is freaking ridiculous!"

My cat had seen them before I did. Just what else is out there? What else have I written off because I thought it was a "fairytale"? What else do animals see that we do not? What else did I embrace as a child, only to be told it was not right, when in all truth it really was real?

The faeries were pleased with my acceptance of them. They asked me not to change anything in the gardens without asking them. After our initial, meeting, I meditated with them often.

Naturally, I was very curious about something that wasn't supposed to exist. I came to know their personalities and even took pictures of their blue orbs with a digital camera. They were an absolute joy; playful, kind and caring. They loved giving me guidance and assistance with the plants.

Since my cat had not yet found a name, I also asked them to find him one.

After a few moments, they whispered a name in my ear: Fineas. It fit.

Fineas is the only cat I have ever known that was given his name by a group of loving faeries. What other wonders are in store?

Shortly after I moved out of the faerie house, I had the opportunity to work with a dog named Granby. His story demonstrates both an animal's entitlement to full disclosure of all that is to happen to them and their ability to overcome and heal through forgiveness and unconditional love.

Granby was a happy-as-can-be Labrador mix. His family loved him and treated him well. Their home was located on a large property where Granby could run freely. He had been roaming a little too far recently so his keepers decided it was in his best interest to have him neutered. He was oblivious about what was going to happen.

As a favor, I took Granby to the clinic for the surgery. I am always happy to help a friend; however, this favor had me feeling a bit apprehensive. Worried for Granby, I decided to do a little preparing with him as I drove him to the clinic. This way he could avoid some fear and confusion.

As we drove, I wondered how much to tell him. At first, he assumed we were going somewhere fun. He enthusiastically hopped in my car with a wag of his tail and a pant of his tongue. I regretfully informed him that this was not going to be a pleasurable experience.

"Granby this isn't a fun trip. You are going in for surgery. Don't worry you will be fine." I bubbled him in protection and asked the Angels to watch over him.

The next day, I went to check on him. He was curled up in his bed, semi-sleeping. I roused Granby gently and asked for permission to help with his healing. He welcomed me.

No longer was Granby oblivious. As I moved my hands into his chakras, I discovered his pain. Larger and more damaging than the pain however, was the confusion, anger, humiliation and violation he was feeling. Additional damage was done because Granby was not informed of his fate. He was traumatized. He stirred to lick his wounds. My heart sunk. I scolded myself for not having the courage to tell him the whole truth: exactly what surgery he would endure. The pain was violently cycling out through my hands. I siphoned it off as quickly and effectively as I could, simultaneously making my apologies. Granby deserved to know. Had I disclosed the complete truth, he would have avoided unnecessary trauma.

As I worked with him, I was reminded of King; he would not even speak about his own castration.

I talked with Granby, explaining that every brave dog and cat has this surgery. I explained that what he did was an act of courage that would allow others like him to find good homes. People did this because there were simply too many dogs. Some were starving and sick, others had no homes. By giving up his ability to make babies, he had given others the chance for health and happiness. Granby accepted this, but with angst. The surgery was too recent. He needed time to heal physically and emotionally.

Granby made a speedy recovery, which we all expected. He thanked me days later when I stopped by for a visit. It was our secret; his keepers knew nothing about what had passed between us. He was adjusting very well and was glad for the work we did. Granby was an exceptionally forgiving dog; he was able to overcome the physical scars of surgery, the emotional scars of the trauma and the mistrust it had caused between him and his keepers. He was an exceptional dog indeed: there are others who never heal from that violation.

The ability to have children is a right. Becoming a parent is a gift. Animals treasure these both. Six was a pig who exemplified this; a "beast" who cherished her children. She lived on a farm as most pigs do. Her recent birth of eight piglets had been very difficult. The farmer had help from veterinarian friends with the delivery. Two of the piglets were stuck in the birth canal. They had to reach in and pull them out.

A few days after the delivery, Six fell terribly ill with a high fever. Her condition was hopeless. The farmer feared the worst. She asked me to tune in to Six to see if we could find out what was wrong.

Six's very first words to me were startling, "I'm going to die tonight."

She barely had the strength to talk with me. There was a gaping leak of energy rushing from her belly. I attempted to seal the energetic hole.

She snapped at me, "No, stop that."

I marveled at her awareness and command over her energy field; she was in full control despite her fear and pain. Realizing I had not asked her permission, I respectfully apologized.

"Six, what happened?"

She showed me a picture of a face I had never met before. A woman was reaching inside, attempting to deliver a piglet. Her reach was too aggressive. She perforated Six's uterus. The enormous energy leak then made sense.

Knowing that she was surely on her way home, I asked her, "Six, what can I do for you?"

"I want to stay. I want to see them grow." She was speaking of her newborns, of course.

"They will be okay. Farmer Jane will take care of them."

She responded sadly, "I will watch them from another plane."

Her comment threw me. How was it that she knew about other planes?

"Is there anything you want me to tell Jane?" I asked.

"Tell her I had fun on the farm."

The farm was not a large commercial operation. It was small, and of quality. Though the animals were viewed as commodities, they were cared for lovingly. Six had a good life.

"Is there was anything else, Six?"

She was so tired. "No."

I prayed over her then, assuring her and asking God for a peaceful passing. I asked the Angels to remove her from pain and reminded her it was all right to go. She was struggling with leaving her babies. We prayed until we felt peace, and then I said good-bye to Six.

The next day, the farmer informed me that Six had passed at around four a.m. Jane was bereaved: she really did love her pigs. I told her what Six said and what I knew to be the cause of death. She fought back her tears. I reminded her that Six would be watching from another plane.

Months later, I visited the now very big and strong piglets. They were growing fast; Jane was a terrific mother. They were happily grunting and stepping over each other in their pen.

There was a presence just to the east of the fence. I concentrated on it. Six was there; she was smiling upon her babies, watching them grow. She directed her love into my heart for a short moment. I felt her gratitude. All was well.

Before meeting Six, I was not aware that animals had a knowledge of the afterlife. I recounted the times when my beloved King would tell me, "You don't see what I see."

What was it that he was seeing?

King also told me he would be watching from somewhere else, just like Six. Both of them had an innate understanding of the heavenly plane; both displayed a wisdom of which I was not privy.

Our own human consciousness is just beginning to awaken to the spiritual truths that animals have already embodied. Perhaps, if we watch, listen and pay close attention we will begin to see what they do.

Afterward

My intention for this book is to bring blessings and love to the animals of this earth. Writing it was so incredibly difficult for me. There were times when I fell to the floor, defeated and unable to continue. In those times, Spirit delivered the grace I needed to persevere. King visited me many times, persuading me to keep writing. He gave me the courage and confidence I needed to bring his book to fruition. I continued with the hope that my readers would receive the same incredible insights about their friends that I received by having lived, loved and worked with my special friend.

Our journey together overflowed with spiritual discovery. King showed me the truth. Our animal friends are spiritual and emotional beings. They hear and understand the thoughts we think. They know what we are feeling and they are busy with thoughts and feelings of their own. They can act as barometers for our lives and struggles, mirroring our states of health. At times, they are attuned to higher spiritual forces than their human counterparts are. Until recently, they have been mistakenly underestimated and taken for granted. Their capability to love unconditionally is both a gift and inspiration. They are a model to which people can aspire. Without overactive egos, animals are free to love completely, without fear clouding their judgments and influencing their actions. Our animal friends can show us the way.

As I reflect on King's life and the wisdom he brought to me, my experiences with other animals come to light. I remember a time when King and I were living in a cabin in the foothills. Several families of bunnies had scattered their homes throughout the bushes outside our front door.

As I stepped out, on my way to work one morning, I spied the tiniest newborn bunny lying just outside of her den. She could have only been a day old. The neighbor cat had raided the den and was scared off before he could finish the job. Carefully, I picked up the tiny baby. She was cold but not wounded: quick action was necessary.

I thought for a moment, "How can I save this tiny, innocent, sweet creature?"

We had to get her core temperature up if she was going to survive. Her best chances would be with her mother; I doubted the Humane Society could help such a young bunny. I held her close to me as I hurried inside to warm up my rice pack. She was smaller than the palm of my hand.

A minute later, we were outside again. I swaddled her in the warm rice pack and placed her just outside the opening of her den. Hopefully she would stay warm there long enough for her mom to come and bring her back to safety. I petted her tiny head and spoke to her softly, "You are loved dear little one. Your mother would be along shortly."

Weeks later, I had forgotten about the bunny rescue. I stepped outside on a lovely spring morning to enjoy the sun and fresh air. Several small bunnies were startled as I moved through the door. They all scampered away except for one. This one hopped and then stopped. He looked at me, studying me for a moment. I kept still. He was looking directly into me.

I heard a small voice in my head, "You're the lady who saved my sister! Thank you."

I was positively astonished.

"Oh, I'm glad to hear she is safe. You're welcome."

With that, the little bunny hopped off after his brothers and sisters. My heart skipped with joy; elated to hear she had made it.

In light of all that King taught me, the bunny rescue has much more significance for me now than it did then. The day that I held the sweet newborn bunny in my hand and the day her brother expressed his love for his sister to me have confirmed a spiritual fact: we are all one.

Through my love and compassion for all living things, I made a choice to intervene to save a precious life. The little boy bunny made a choice to move past his fear of humans and connect to me in gratitude. A "wild" animal recognized my value for all of life and my acknowledgment of God in all things. We were not so different that day, and we are not so different now. He is no more wild than I am and I am no less wild then he is. The same creator made us both, in love. Our values are the same. Life, love, family, food, safety and fun; we are cut from the same cloth, just sewn a little differently.

Another experience I had with a young border collie is brought to my mind as I finish this labor of love. This experience illustrates the importance of placing value and reverence on the lives of our animal friends. This was a day that I witnessed the mistreatment of an animal that I could not understand or look upon without intervening.

In my early twenties, I spent a summer working on an organic farm in the thumb of Michigan. I had only been there a few days when I began to notice how the animals were viewed. The general vibe of the farm held no real value for life. This farm viewed animals as commodities; cash crops.

One particular afternoon, after I finished all my work, I was enjoying a stroll around the backside of the farmer's property. I stumbled upon an old silo. The silo was repurposed as a pen for the farmer's border collies. I looked through the fencing and the view dropped me to my knees. The reality of what my eyes were showing me cut my heart like a knife. Several dead puppies were lying about the perimeter of the pen. I ran to inspect each one, hoping for signs of life. Why had the farmers not mentioned they had puppies? I didn't even know they were there!

I approached the last body with tears streaming down my face. How could this happen? How had they all died? I knelt over the little body, reaching my hand through the fence to check for warmth. She moved! Her breathing was labored; she was weak but alive. I pulled her from the pen and ran to find the farmer.

Cradling her in my arms, I angrily questioned, "What is this? The rest are dead! How could you let this happen? You did not even tell me you had puppies! We have to save her!"

The farmer scolded his fourteen-year-old son, "You were responsible for feeding and watering these pups. They are income!" He went inside to phone the vet.

My eyes shot penetrating fire at the farmer's irresponsible son.

The farmer soon returned with the news that the vet wanted one hundred dollars to put the pup on IV fluids. The farmer would not justify the cost. The pups were supposed to make money not cost money: he refused to approve the expense. He saw no value saving this puppy's life.

Enraged and disgusted, I took matters into my own hands. Inside the house, I found some beef stock and an eyedropper. Outside, in the warm sun, with that tiny puppy in my lap, I labored to keep her alive. Every ten minutes, I gave her a dropper full of salty stock only to watch her throw it up moments later.

During my attempts to get fluid in her body, I stared into her eyes. Into my consciousness flowed the picture of her watching all of her brothers and sisters die. She would be the last to go. Her eyes hinted at her relief that she would not die alone.

For two hours, I worked and prayed, begging that she would keep some fluid down. She was so tired, so weak, so exhausted. She was giving up.

I pleaded with her and God. Peace blanketed us. A strong knowing came over me; she needed to rest. I moved her into the shady stall, made her comfortable, petted her and told her she was loved. As I closed the door, I promised to check on her in just a few minutes.

The disgust, grief and horror I felt had me packing my things. I would not be a part of a farm or a family who did not value life.

The few things I had were thrown hastily into my truck. I was done! My head was screaming silent obscenities at the farmer, his farm and his family.

I pulled my truck up to the stall where I had left the dying pup. As soon as I opened the stall door, I knew she had gone. My hands felt her body for breathing. She was not there anymore. More tears spilled as anger and grief moved their way through me. I apologized to the pup on behalf of everyone. She deserved so much better.

The sounds of my tires peeling brought the farmer out of his door, "Where are you going, Kerry?"

"You people have no respect for life! I will not be a part of it. Good-bye."

The words I spoke were tame compared to the rage I was feeling. I wanted to scream terrible things at the farmer. Instead, I let my actions speak for me. I never saw the farmer, his family or that farm again.

That experience came at a time in my life when I could not allow myself to believe that what passed between me and that puppy were real. I assumed that I had imagined her gratitude and the entire experience was brushed under a rug.

As I reflect on the moments I spent with the border collie puppy, I understand now that everything that passed between us was not just my imagination. When I gazed into that puppy's eyes, her gratitude was definite. She did show me the picture of her watching her siblings die and she certainly was afraid. In her last moments, even though I could not save her, she felt loved and received the comfort she deserved.

As I look back, on all of my time spent with my animal friends, it seems rediculous that I ever thought any experience was only imagination.

By writing this book, I have sent a beacon out into the world. I am asking for change. King and I have a vision for the world, which includes you and your guardians living side by side with mutual respect and compassion for each other. King and I envision all animals receiving the best treatment, with no cruelty, abuse or neglect. We hope you will recognize your friends as the divine gifts from God that they really are. Let their love teach and inspire you.

Now is the time for you to open your heart to the truth. A new door has opened for you; walk through it! Get to know your friends! Listen to them! Pay attention! They are all patiently waiting to tell you something.